INSIGHT ⦿ GUIDES

EXPLORE

WARSAW

⊙ Walking Eye App

YOUR FREE EBOOK AVAILABLE THROUGH THE WALKING EYE APP

Your guide now includes a free eBook to your chosen destination, for the same great price as before. Simply download the Walking Eye App from the App Store or Google Play to access your free eBook.

HOW THE WALKING EYE APP WORKS

Through the Walking Eye App, you can purchase a range of eBooks and destination content. However, when you buy this book, you can download the corresponding eBook for free. Just see below in the grey panel where to find your free content and then scan the QR code at the bottom of this page.

Destinations: Download essential destination content featuring recommended sights and attractions, restaurants, hotels and an A–Z of practical information, all available for purchase.

Ships: Interested in ship reviews? Find independent reviews of river and ocean ships in this section, all available for purchase.

eBooks: You can download your free accompanying digital version of this guide here. You will also find a whole range of other eBooks, all available for purchase.

Free access to travel-related blog articles about different destinations, updated on a daily basis.

HOW THE EBOOKS WORK

The eBooks are provided in EPUB file format. Please note that you will need an eBook reader installed on your device to open the file. Many devices come with this as standard, but you may still need to install one manually from Google Play.

The eBook content is identical to the content in the printed guide.

HOW TO DOWNLOAD THE WALKING EYE APP

1. Download the Walking Eye App from the App Store or Google Play.
2. Open the app and select the scanning function from the main menu.
3. Scan the QR code on this page – you will then be asked a security question to verify ownership of the book.
4. Once this has been verified, you will see your eBook in the purchased ebook section, where you will be able to download it.

Other destination apps and eBooks are available for purchase separately or are free with the purchase of the Insight Guide book.

CONTENTS

FOODIES

The Warsaw gastronomic revolution is in full swing, so it's worth checking out its hotspots, including Koszyki (route 9), Saska Kępa (route 7) and Grzybowski Square (route 8).

RECOMMENDED ROUTES FOR...

HISTORY AFICIONADOS

Learn about Warsaw's extraordinary history at one of these excellent museums: the Museum of Warsaw (route 1), the Warsaw Uprising Museum (route 8) and the Museum of the History of Polish Jews (route 8).

MUSIC LOVERS

Discover Frederick Chopin's Warsaw (routes 3, 6 and 7) and hear his music being played in the beautiful surroundings of Łazienki Park on Sunday afternoons (route 6).

NATURE LOVERS

Escape the city and immerse yourself in one of Warsaw's green oases, from elegant Łazienki (route 6) or Ujazdowski (route 5) parks and Krasiński (route 2) or Saski (route 3) Gardens to the wilder Skaryszewski (route 14).

NIGHT OWLS

Get carried away at one of the clubs on the left riverbank (routes 9 and 7) or head across the river for the more underground feel of Prague's 11 Listopada street (route 12).

SCIENCE BUFFS

Want to see the state-of-the art planetarium and discover the secret of light? Head to the Copernicus Science Centre (route 7) or visit the Museum of Maria Skłodkowska-Curie in the New Town (route 2).

SHOPAHOLICS

Take a walk along Mokotowska street (route 9) – an excellent hunting ground for the best Polish designer clothes, or embark on a shopping spree in the exclusive stores around Three Crosses Square (route 5).

SOCIALIST-REALISM FANS

Admire the monumental Constitution Square, a classic example of the Socialist-realist style (route 9) or lose yourself in communist nostalgia at the Palace of Culture (route 9) and the Neon Museum (route 14).

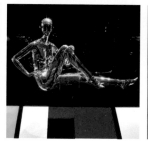

INTRODUCTION

An introduction to Warsaw's geography, customs and culture, plus illuminating background information on cuisine, history and what to do when you're there.

New skyscrapers punctuate Warsaw's skyline

EXPLORE WARSAW

Warsaw is a fast-changing, modern city with a rich, though turbulent, past. Despite the fact its allure may not be immediate, it has plenty of scenic corners and places of historic significance that will send tingles down your spine.

Poland's proud capital for over 400 years, Warsaw is a bustling city which has reinvented itself as a tourist destination as well as Central Europe's financial hub. High-rise glass and steel buildings contrast with the luscious green of its numerous parks and squares, while the city's long and often bitter history has left a lasting imprint on its architecture, producing an eclectic mix of contrasting architectural styles, from the monolithic Palace of Culture and Science to the quaint streets of the Old Town.

Enormous changes since the 1989 democratic elections and Poland's accession to the EU in 2004 have turned Warsaw into a thoroughly European, metropolitan capital. Cafés are full of people enjoying leisurely coffee and cake breaks, bars and restaurants are packed with power-suited business people, and a growing number of shops stock everything from Cartier, Versace and exotic foodstuffs, to local specialities such as folk crafts. The city has a thriving nightlife scene with numerous bars and nightclubs, particularly in the centre and, in summer, along the riverside.

GEOGRAPHY AND LAYOUT

Warsaw lies in the heart of the Mazovia region in central Poland, on the banks of the River Vistula (Wisła). Unlike most other European capitals, it doesn't have a proper 'centre' and the entire city, along with its numerous attractions, is spread across a large area of 517 sq km (200 sq miles), posing a serious challenge even for the most hardened walkers. Fortunately, the modern public transport system – including trams, buses and a shiny metro – is efficient, punctual and easy to use even for people with a minimal knowledge of Polish. Licensed taxis and Uber cars, as well as Veturilo city bike stations, are also omnipresent in the greater city centre.

HISTORY

While the exact origins of Warsaw have eluded historians, one legend states that an amalgamation of the names of the fisherman Wars and Sawa, who lived by the Vistula river, provided a name for the city. Another legend states that a mermaid swimming in the Vistula told

Old Town buildings

Mazovian fishermen of an indestructible city that would be founded there. Warsaw has certainly fulfilled the mermaid's prophecy, with the city's history being a continual cycle of invasion, destruction, rebuilding and resurrection.

The Old Town evolved around the residence of the Mazovian dukes, established on the site of the present Royal Castle in 1281. The city's evolution continued on the basis of its key position on trade routes through Poland. Moreover, Mazovia was also growing in importance as the central point between the two capitals of the Polish-Lithuanian Commonwealth, Kraków and Vilnius.

Parliament first met in Warsaw in 1529, and from 1573 royal elections were held here (the king being elected rather than hereditary). However, the king continued to reside in Kraków, the capital of Poland since 1040, until King Zygmunt III Waza proclaimed Warsaw the capital city in 1596.

Between 1655 and 1660 the Swedish invasion, known as 'Potop' ('The Deluge') devastated Poland, and seriously depleted Warsaw's buildings and population. However, under King Jan III Sobieski – elected in 1674 – the city enjoyed great prosperity, with numerous buildings, palaces and principal thoroughfares dating from this time, including the king's summer residence, Wilanów, on the outskirts of the city.

During the period of the Enlightenment, in the second half of the 18th century, commerce and culture evolved rapidly, which included the founding of the National Theatre and several periodicals, while the first constitution in Europe was ratified in Warsaw on 3 May 1791.

However, three successive partitions of Poland, beginning in 1772, saw the country progressively divided between Prussia, Austria-Hungary and Russia. Initially placed under Prussian rule, Napoleon then established the city as the capital of the Grand Duchy of Warsaw. Following the Congress of Vienna in 1815, Warsaw became capital of the Congress Kingdom of Poland, ruled by the Tsar of Russia. Warsaw was also at the centre of numerous insurrections during this time, with the uprisings of 1830 and 1863 the most significant. When Poland achieved independence as a sovereign nation in 1918, following World War I and the rollback of Russian and German forces, Warsaw retained its status as capital.

One of the most tragic periods in the city's turbulent history was World War II, with more than 700,000 citizens killed during the German Occupation, including the city's vibrant Jewish population. After the Warsaw Uprising, Hitler ordered that the Poles be punished, by razing Warsaw to the ground. The city was systematically destroyed and left virtually uninhabited, with the total wartime damage resulting in almost 85 percent of the city being reduced to rubble. A massive post-war rebuilding programme recreated the Old Town and New Town districts, as well as numer-

All Saints Church, Grzybowski Square

ous palaces, churches and important civic buildings. Ironically, the Communist regime that took over post-War demolished 19th-century mansion blocks and tenement buildings in the centre of Warsaw, which had survived the Nazi regime, and converted this area into a 'showpiece' of Socialist Realism architecture.

The wartime legacy means that various poignant sites are marked throughout the city. There are numerous plaques set on walls and pavements, stating when and how many Poles were executed on each site by the Nazis, with candles and flowers still placed by many of these memorials. The Old Town and adjacent New Town took around 30 years to reconstruct – this was carried out so authentically that both were awarded Unesco World Heritage status. If you didn't know the history you'd never guess they were reproductions.

Over the last few years, the city has experienced a meteoric rise with sleek high rise buildings and hotels springing up in the centre, and new housing estates, modern museums, bridges, metro lines, stadiums, cycling routes and river boulevards constructed. Several international events have been held in the Polish capital, including Euro 2012 football matches, a UN Climate Conference and a NATO summit. As the ubiquitous tower cranes attest, the construction spree continues, boosting optimism and local pride.

CLIMATE

The best time to visit Warsaw is late spring, summer (although it could be rather wet) or the famous 'golden Polish autumn' (Sept–mid-Oct) when days are still relatively long and warm while parks and forests explode with all shades of red, yellow and brown as tree leaves begin to change colour. This time of the year is also relatively dry.

However, it should be noted that the Polish climate is quite unpredictable – even in mid-summer there could be rainy days when the temperature drops to 13–15°C, so it's always wise to have a jumper, umbrella or a raincoat to hand. On the other hand, summers in Warsaw can also be suffocatingly hot, so pack light cotton garments if travelling at this time of the year.

In winter expect more rain than snow and temperatures around 0°C for most of the time (albeit some days could be much colder than that). Taking a warm coat, sturdy, water-resistant boots and wool trousers is advisable. People in Warsaw tend to be style-conscious, so put on elegant clothes (such as jackets and dresses) if you plan to attend the theatre or opera, or have a dinner at an exclusive restaurant. For an up-to-date weather forecast go to www.pogodynka.pl.

PEOPLE

Varsovians (people from Warsaw) are caricatured as being fast-talking, fast-

Warsaw's Metro   *Sunset over a River Vistula beach*

driving, corporate climbers who consider themselves superior to the rest of the country. The fact is, however, that only about half of the city's inhabitants were born in Warsaw. Each year thousands of Poles from all regions arrive in search of job opportunities and a better life. The locals call them *słoiki* (jars), because allegedly, they return to their home towns or villages every weekend and bring back plenty of food in jars. As inhabitants of other big cities, Varsovi-

DON'T LEAVE WARSAW WITHOUT...

Seeing the Old Town. Having a stroll along the narrow, cobbled streets of the Old Town on a sunny day is one of the most pleasant things to do in Warsaw. Even crowds of tourists can not spoil the magical charm of this part of the city. Hard to believe, but the present Old Town is a reconstruction from the 1950s, based on pre-war sketches. See page 30.

Visiting the Palace of Culture (Pałac Kultury). Although Varsovians have ambivalent feelings about the city's highest building (42 floors, soon to be overtaken by the Varso Tower), considered by many to be a symbol of the post-war Soviet domination, it is definitely worth popping in if only to have a look at opulent interiors or to take a lift to the observation deck, which offers superb views of the city. See page 80.

Listening to Chopin's music. Capturing the very essence of Polish soul, hearing music composed by Frederick Chopin is one of the city's main attractions and can be heard at many venues where Chopin recitals are regularly organised, both open-air and indoor. See page 25.

Learning about Warsaw's history. Painful and gruesome though it may be, the city's history is a fascinating tale of a cycle of destruction and revival that has left an indelible imprint on the city and its inhabitants' minds. Learn more about it at two excellent museums: the Warsaw Uprising Museum and the Museum of Warsaw. See pages 35 and 73.

Trying a *pączek*. The fluffy *pączek* (doughnut) filled with rose jam is the ultimate delight for those with sweet tooth. Some of the best are served at Blikle Café on Nowy Świat street. See page 52.

Getting to know Jewish Warsaw. With the Museum of the History of Polish Jews now open and the ever-popular Festival of Jewish Culture celebrated every September, the revival of Jewish culture in Warsaw is in full swing. See page 71.

Having a stroll by the river. The city's riverbanks are the place to be in summer. Cycling and walking paths, beaches and dozens of bars, clubs and cafés scattered along the Vistula draw crowds of people day and night. See page 65.

Visiting Praga. Take a stroll through scenic Praga, where the old tenements ooze the irresistible charm of pre-war Warsaw, and explore its quickly gentrifying quarters with its trendy clubs and restaurants. See page 91.

ans, particularly younger ones, tend to lead hectic lives: they work (or study) long hours during the day, while at night they unwind with friends over a glass of wine or beer at one of the atmospheric bars or cafés. Always in a rush, they are often seen as inconsiderate or even rude. However, on the whole, these stereotypes quickly vanish once you get to know people better.

LOCAL TIMINGS

Being in a hurry is a permanent feature of Varsovians. Nevertheless, they manage to squeeze some time for a proper sit-down lunch (which is more like dinner in Poland), which is usually taken around 2 or 3pm. A light supper, often enjoyed at home, is usually eaten between 6 and 8pm.

If you can, try to go shopping on a weekday as commercial centres and shops are usually packed with throngs of people at weekends. Do not plan visits to the city's museums on Mondays, as is this is when they are usually closed.

City residents are also obsessed with healthy living —you can see them jogging at the most extreme hours of the day and night. Cycling, swimming and playing football are also popular.

POLITICS AND ECONOMICS

The process of re-privatisation of the land and buildings which were nationalized after 1945 by the communist regime, has resulted in many irregularities and become a hot political issue in recent years. Shady legal practices, unethical links between some city officials, prominent lawyers and developers as well as upfront allegations of corruption have blemished the otherwise impressive record of Warsaw's first female mayor Hanna Gronkiewicz Waltz from the centre-right Civic Platform (PO) party, who has held power in the city since 2006.

Despite these issues, the city has experienced an unprecedented boom in the last decade with skyscrapers springing up around the Palace of Culture, main streets being revamped and the entire quarters of the city rapidly changing. The construction of the second metro line that will span western and eastern parts of the city is well under way with a large section already in operation. Old boroughs like Praga are being revitalised and populated by newcomers who bring along new trends, habits and customs, thus creating an even richer social fabric. And since the right-wing Law and Justice Party (PiS) assumed national power in 2015, the capital has once again become vocally political, with marches organised on regular basis both against and in support of the current government. While cherishing its rich history, Warsaw — driven by the dynamism of its residents — incessantly looks forward in search of new opportunities and challenges.

The Old Town square at night, lined with restaurants

TOP TIPS FOR VISITING WARSAW

Get a Warsaw Pass. A great way to save some złotys and skip the line to the city's main attractions, the pass comes in three versions: 24, 48 and 72 hours (www.warsawpass.com). It also includes a free hop-on hop-off bus tour and can be combined with a public transport ticket.

Take in a free concert. When in Warsaw in summer, try not to miss the excellent free recitals of Chopin music at Łazienki Park or the best jazz musicians playing in the Old Town's square. These are just a few of several musical events which are available to the public for free (http://warsawnow.pl)

Hop aboard bus no 180. This bus route covers the most attractions in Warsaw, from Wilanów Palace in the south through the Royal Route and the Old Town to the Jewish heritage sites in Muranów, and eventually to the Jewish cemetery. You can buy a one day ticket (see page 124) and use the bus as an excellent hop-on hop-off tour.

Go to the National Opera/National Theatre. The Warsaw Opera/National Theatre is known for excellent performances including top-class national and international artists. Ticket prices are substantially cheaper than to other famous operas, while its artistic director Mariusz Treliński gained international fame by skillfully blending the classical genre with current aesthetic trends.

Get a Chopin Pass. The Chopin Pass entitles you to visit both Chopin museums as well as get a free transfer to/from Żelazowa Wola (54 kilometers from Warsaw).

Buy it online (www.chopinpass.pl; Apr–Oct; in winter call tel. 0533 493 940; 119 zł), or at the ticket offices of the Fryderyk Chopin Museum and the Palace of Culture. Comfortable minibuses – equipped with a collection of Chopin music – take up to 8 people and leave from the parking lot in front of the Tourist Office in the Palace of Culture (next to the Congress Hall). In summer, Chopin recitals are also held in Żelazowa Wola on Sat and Sun at noon and 3pm.

Hit the food markets. A must for all food-conscious tourists, Warsaw's food markets boast the best products Poland has to offer. From excellent breads and organic vegetables to cold meats and smoked fish from the Mazurian lakes, the city markets are simply a must for foodies (see page 18).

Try tripe soup in Lotos. If you want to try quintessential Warsaw cuisine head to one of the 'old' restaurants such as Lotos in Dolny Mokotów for an excellent tripe soup or tongue in aspic. The amazing late-1970s interior is yet another reason to visit the place.

Take a tram. Trams are excellent for moving around the city on weekdays, when even public buses may be slowed down by the traffic jams. They are modern, clean, safe and – unlike the metro – let you discover the city while commuting.

Relax in a park. Leave the city's bustle behind and immerse yourself in one of these green oases that stretch from north to south across town: Saski i Krasińskich Garden, Skaryszewski i Ujazdowski Parks or Łazienki.

Pierogi are dumplings and Poland's most famous food

FOOD AND DRINK

In recent years Warsaw has experienced a gastronomic revolution, with excellent bars and restaurants springing up everywhere. The best thing is that prices at even the best establishments are substantially lower than in other major capital cities.

Polish cuisine ranges from rich and substantial to light and elegant. Long gone are days when every restaurant in Warsaw would only serve one of the national soups: *barszcz* (beetroot), *żurek* (sour rye), *rosół* (chiken broth) or *pomidorowa* (tomato), followed by the classic *schabowy z kapustą* (breaded pork chops with braised cabbage), *mielone* (fried meatballs), *bigos* (braised cabbage and sauerkraut with meats and wild mushrooms) or the iconic *pierogi* (dumplings).

Since the mid-1990s, Warsaw has spearheaded a Polish culinary revolution. However, it wasn't until 2013 that chef Wojciech Modest Amaro identified the perfect blend of fresh Polish seasonal produce, creativity and perfectly mastered modern cooking techniques and was rewarded with Poland's first Michelin star for his restaurant Atelier Amaro (see page 118). Today, the capital's culinary scene offers quality dining options from every corner of the world with plenty of Asian (Vietnamese, Chinese, Indian and Thai), Italian, French, Spanish, Balkan, Mexican, Turkish and, naturally, Polish restaurants to choose from.

Poles tend to start a day with a hearty breakfast which may include scrambled or boiled eggs, cottage cheese, yellow cheese, cold meats and or/cereals. The main meal of the day is a three course, late lunch (2–3pm) usually comprising a soup, main dish and dessert followed by a cup of tea or coffee. Dinner is usually eaten at home around 6–7pm and features open sandwiches (*kanapki*).

LOCAL CUISINE

Only a few traditional Varsovian dishes have survived into the present day. A radical transformation of the city's population make-up after World War II as well as the effects of rationing and frequent food shortages in the communist era resulted in many old recipes being abandoned. Only a few simple, mostly peasants' plates endured. The most famous of these include *flaki* (tripe soup), *pyzy* (potato dumplings), *karp po żydowsku* (Jewish style carp) and *schab po warszawsku* (Warsaw style pork loin). Young chefs have revived some of the old recipes, after giving them a modern revamp, so it is now possible to find such nose-to-tail delicacies on the menus as *grasica* (thymus), *móżdżek* (brains) or *cynaderki* (kidneys).

Zoladkowa Gorzka vodka

Pierogi (dumplings) are the most famous Polish foodstuff and have become an internationally recognisable staple of the cuisine. *Pierogi* are prepared by placing a small amount of stuffing in a circle of dough, which is then folded over and sealed with a scalloped edge. The most popular fillings include cheese, mashed potatoes and sautéed onion (called *ruskie* which means 'Russian'); cabbage and sautéed mushrooms (*z kapustą i grzybami*), and minced meat (*z mięsem*).

Polish cuisine, in the past heavily influenced by German, Austrian, Jewish, Russian and even Turkish culinary traditions, has undergone a major change as lighter dishes are now made with local produce or freshly picked ingredients including wild mushrooms, herbs, forest fruits, game meat and locally caught fish. A growing number of widely acclaimed Polish chefs – often with experience from the world's best restaurants – have unleashed their creativity to revolutionise Polish cuisine and adapt it to modern standards. Vegetarian and vegan options abound, with healthy living evermore encouraged. Indeed, Warsaw has one of the largest number of restaurants serving exclusively vegan dishes of all the European capitals. Gluten-free establishments are also fashionable.

WHERE TO EAT

Restaurants
Warsaw has recently become a gastronomic mecca with restaurants to suit all tastes and wallets. Top-notch, high-end establishments concentrate mostly in the city centre and include two Michelin-starred trailblazing restaurants: Senses and Atelier Amaro (see page 118). You can also choose from a great variety of mid-range restaurants where the food quality is equally good or even better than at the more hyped establishments.

You will be spoilt for choice when it comes to ethnic restaurants category, with a varied choice of bars or restaurants on almost every corner, at least in the city centre. The culinary influx began with the arrival of cheap Vietnamese eateries and was quickly followed by excellent Italian pizzerias, Japanese sushi parlours, sophisticated French restaurants, Indian curry joints, Mexican taquerias and Middle Eastern falafel and kebab stands, as well as wonderful Georgian bars.

Street food
Even fast food has experienced a transformation, with the old zapiekankas (grilled baguettes with cheese, mushrooms and lots of ketchup), popular in communist times, superseded by Western (McDonalds, Pizza Hut) or Polish chains (Bobby Burger). The latest craze, however, are food trucks, offering a variety of street eats ranging from Cuban grilled sandwiches to artisan burgers or salads, which can be found in dozens of locations across town (in summer, numerous trucks gather in the so called Food Port on the left riverbank near Pon-

At a milk bar in Praga

iatowski bridge). You can also find out where your favourite food truck is located by downloading the TruckMe app.

Milk bars

Bary mleczne (milk bars) are now almost a thing of the past but if you can find one, they make a good alternative to restaurants and are excellent value for money. Mainly self-service, cafeteria-style, they occupy simple premises and have a choice of basic dishes including all kinds of dumplings and pancakes as well as soups and classic meatballs. Often you get a home-cooked and filling plate for very little.

Cafés

Many Varsovians can't imagine starting a day without a cup of good coffee, and they tend to be fussy about their cup. The number of cafés and knowledgeable baristas have shot up over the last few years and caffeine addicts can now choose from big international chains' outlets such as the stylish Green Caffè Nero (www.greencaffenero.pl) or Star-

bucks, or small, independent coffee bars with their own roasters, who source coffee beans directly from the world's best producers.

Bread and pastries

Polish bread, be it a nutritious rye bread or a freshly baked crunchy white roll, deservedly enjoys an excellent reputation. Even large Polish chain bakeries (Lubaszka or Grzybek) churn out decent products. Visitors with sweet tooth will also appreciate the mouth-watering traditional cakes and sweets. Many of them, such as *napoleonki* (millefeuille) end *eklerki* (eclairs) originally arrived from France, while others such as *wuzetka* (a delicious combination of chocolate sponge layered with whipped cream) were invented in Warsaw. The classic Polish cakes sold in every pastry shop and bakery include *sernik* (cheesecake) and *makowiec* (a sponge cake rolled around a filling of poppy seeds with honey and raisins). During carnival, and particularly on Fat Thursday (last Thursday before Lent), try *pączki* (doughnuts) with rose jam and *faworki* (angel wings).

Food and drink prices

Throughout this book, the price categories for a two-course meal for one without drinks are:

€€€€ = over 70zł
€€€ = 50–70zł
€€ = 30–50zł
€ = up to 30zł

Food and breakfast markets

The fashionable *bazary* (food markets) and *targi śniadaniowe* (breakfast markets) usually offer freshly made juices, organic fruits and vegetables, cheeses, cold meats and fresh or smoked fish. There is also plenty of finger food and snacks to tempt your palate. The breakfast markets are held at spring and sum-

Sizzling sausages for sale   *Modern chefs are bringing Warsaw's food scene up to date*

mer weekends in several places across town. For details, check their website: http://targsniadaniowy.pl.

Bazary traditionally include dozens of stands under one roof, offering a variety of food, bread, fresh produce and even regular cafés or bars, and stay open throughout the year. Some of the most popular are Bazar Olkuska (www.bazarolkuska. pl), Hala Mirowska and Biobazar (http://biobazar.org.pl) on Żelazna street in the former Norblin factory.

DRINKS

Tea

Never mind the coffee culture explosion, tea (*herbata*) is still one of the favourite beverages of Warsaw residents. And even if there are not any tea rooms in the area, every respectable café will have a large selection of green, black, white and fruit/herbal teas to choose from. In Warsaw, tea is usually taken without milk.

Vodka

The origin of the Polish national drink, *wódka* (the name comes from woda or water), has been the object of a long-standing dispute between Poles and Russians. One thing is certain: the earliest recorded use of the word is on a Polish document dating from 1405. Polish vodkas come in a variety of flavours and strengths and can be made from cereals or potatoes (there are also blended vodkas). The most popular brands include Żubrówka, which has a

blade of wild grass from the Białowieża forest inside the bottle, Wyborowa, Krupnik and Żytnia. High-end vodkas include Chopin and Belvedere. A popular way of getting acquainted with vodka is to try it at one of numerous bars scattered across the centre serving the drink, paired with a specific range of specialities called *zakąski* (literally, nibbles) including salted herring fillets, pork jelly, beef tartare, cold meats and rye bread.

Beer, mead and wine

With the arrival of craft breweries, Polish beer scene experienced a dramatic change. Once dominated by huge state companies (Żywiec and Okocim are good examples), which have been taken over by big international companies, there are now a mind-blowing number of artisanal beers that can satisfy even the most picky connoisseurs. You can try them in one of classic beer pubs such as Cuda na Kiju or Same Krafty (see page 122).

Mead (honey wine) is one of the earliest alcoholic drinks prepared by the Slavs. It is kept hot by serving it in ceramic beakers that stand on a tray heated by a small candle. One of the best places to try it in Warsaw is Pasieka restaurant in the New Town.

Wine, which for many years was expensive and of poor quality, has enjoyed a similar revival as beer. Now it usually accompanies meals and is drunk regularly by a growing number of locals who are spoilt for choice by the elegant wine bars that have sprung up across town.

Amber jewellery for sale

SHOPPING

With a mind-dazzling number of shops, ranging from small outlets to huge modern shopping centres, Warsaw is a shopper's paradise. Numerous concept stores cater for conscious buyers looking for originality and top-class quality.

Warsaw's traditional shopping streets are Marszałkowska, Chmielna and Nowy Świat but many up-and-coming shopping areas have emerged in recent years, including the Mokotowska street, Three Crosses square, The Mysia and Bracka streets. They are lined with elegant boutiques and designer shops selling the most fashionable attire.

JEWELLERY

The most popular souvenir bought in Warsaw is amber jewellery, often set in silver and readily available from shops in the Old Town including Art Gallery Amber Silver Line (www.warsawamber.pl), Galeria Bursztynek (www.bursztynek.co) and Art Studio Jewellery Schubert (www.worldofamber.pl). Also worth a visit are stores offering modern hand-made jewellery by well-known Polish designers. These include Lewanowicz (www.lewanowicz.com) with three branches across town, including the Złote Tarasy shopping centre (see below), Galeria Metal in the Old Town market square, Ania Kruk (https://aniakruk.pl) on Mokotowska street and Orska at Mysia (http://orska.pl).

FOR FOOD LOVERS

Polish vodka (see Food and Drink) could be another good souvenir to bring home from Warsaw; it is available on virtually every corner (it is hard to believe there is a city with more spirits shops per square meter than Poland's capital). Another Polish speciality are *nalewki* (fruit-flavoured liquors); the best are home-made but those sold under the Soplica brand are not bad either.

There are plenty of sweets and delicacies that you might want to take back home from Warsaw. For high-quality sausages, cold cuts, dumplings, pâtés, liquors and many more head to Krakowski Kredens (www.krakowskikredens.pl), which has branches in nearly all major commercial centres. Famous fudge from Milanówek factory (http://zpcmilanowek.pl) is widely available in sweet shops, as are chocolates made in Warsaw's Wedel Factory (www.wedel.com). A good place to try top-class Wedel chocolates, besides excellent hot chocolate, is the old-fashioned shop at Wedel's Chocolate Lounge (www.wedelpijalnie.pl) on Szpitalna 8. Although not a Warsaw speci-

Złote Tarasy   *At Grzybowski Square flea market*

ality, *Śliwki Nałęczowskie* (chocolates filled with plums) are another sweet delicacy worth trying.

SHOPPING CENTRES AND DEPARTMENT STORES

Warsaw has top-class commercial centres which get very crowded at weekends when entire families descend hunting for bargains, to see a film at the cinema and have a family dinner. The biggest and most popular are: Złote Tarasy (Złota 59 street; http://zlotetarasy.pl) with a futuristic undulating glass roof, located next to the Central Railway Station and the Palace of Culture; Arkadia at the Radosława Roundabout (Aleja Jana Pawła II 82; http://arkadia.com.pl), which is the biggest in the entire country and still being expanded; and the posh Galeria Mokotów (http://galeriamokotow.pl) on Wołoska 12 street. Its Designers' Gallery (including both world famous and national designers' boutiques) is a favourite hunting ground for aspiring fashionistas. The newest centre is the Plac Unii City Shopping (www.placunii.pl) featuring over 50 shops and a cult Supersam foodstore in the basement.

Centrally located Vitkac (Bracka 9 street; www.vitkac.com) is the most exclusive department store in Warsaw, featuring designers such as Louis Vuitton, Balenciaga, Alexander McQueen, Kenzo and Stella McCartney, to name just a few. Large commercial centres in the capital are open daily from 10am to 10pm, with an earlier closing on Sundays.

WARSAW ANTIQUE MARKETS

Bazar na Kole (Koło market) is Warsaw's oldest and one of the biggest antique outdoor markets in Poland. A true paradise for lovers of old things and vintage collectors, it is located in the Wola district at 99 Obozowa street. Here you will find beautiful period furniture, stamps, watches, clocks, pottery, glass, silver, paintings and posters as well as old military helmets and sabers. The market operates every Sat and Sun from 6am–3pm, but it is best to arrive early (8am at the latest), soon after the sellers have unpacked and put all their treasures on display.

Bargain hard and beware of fakes. The Koło market is very popular with both tourists and locals (particularly in summer months), sometimes you may even spot Polish celebrities hunting for an original present or a knick-knack.

Alternatively, head for the ZOO flea market (Sat–Sun 11am–5pm) on the right bank of the Vistula river at Aleja Solidarności 55 in the Praga district. Easily accessible by metro (Dworzec Wileński station) or tram (Park Praski stop), it boasts modern design from the 1950s, 1960s and 1970s, comic strips, vintage fashion, antique books, vinyls, home décor and much more. Gourmets will be delighted to find food stands with local delicacies.

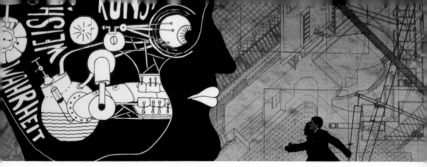

'The Magic Flute' at the Teatr Wielki Opera Narodowa

ENTERTAINMENT

Warsaw is quite simply a hedonist's dream. There are pubs, bars, discos, clubs, theatres and live music venues to choose from, so finding something to do when the sun goes down will not be difficult.

As far as entertainment is concerned, in Warsaw you are spoilt for choice. Whether you want to attend a top-class opera or ballet performance, a jazz concert in one of the atmospheric clubs or head to a wild rave party by the river, Warsaw will satisfy even the most demanding visitors. In addition to the city centre – including the area around Nowy Świat, Mazowiecka and Piłsudski square – you will find pockets of excellent clubs and bars in the Prague (Mińska and 11 Listopada streets), Powiśle (River Bank), Saska Kępa or Mokotów. The recently opened Koszyki (www.koszyki.com; see page 85), has become a major magnet for the city's bohemians.

OPERA AND THEATRE

Known for top-quality entertainment, Teatr Wielki Opera Narodowa (the Grand Theatre National Opera; http://teatr wielki.pl) features the best opera and ballet performances in town. If the Polish National Opera is performing *Halka* during your stay, do try to get a ticket. Even if you cannot understand a word of Polish, you will still be able to follow this sad love story about a poor girl from the mountains. The finest musicals in Warsaw can be enjoyed at the Roma (www. teatrroma.pl) and Rampa (www.teatr-rampa.pl) musical theatres. Concerts of classical music can be heard at the Warsaw Philharmonic (http://filharmonia. pl), Fryderyk Chopin University of Music (www.chopin.edu.pl), the Warsaw Chamber Opera (www.operakameralna.pl) and every Friday at the Copernicus Science Centre's planetarium.

Varsovians are avid theatre goers and can choose from a variety of drama ranging from productions of classical works by both Polish and international dramatists to contemporary experimental plays. The latter are represented by acclaimed directors such as Krzysztof Warlikowski who stages widely popular plays (with English subtitles, early booking essential) in the Nowy Teatr (www.nowyteatr.org).

TICKETS AND INFORMATION

Information about all cultural events can be found in Friday's *Co jest grane* supplement to the *Gazeta Wyborcza*, including everything you want to know about the latest films, exhibitions and performances taking place in Warsaw. There

Vistula beachside club

are also a few excellent websites (in English) with the latest news: www.kulturalna.warszawa.pl, www.culture.pl and www.warsawvoice.pl. Tickets for theatres, concerts and all cultural events can be bought at major hotels, theatre box offices, Empik bookstores and online: www.ebilet.pl, www.eventim.pl, www.ticketpro.pl.

JAZZ AND MUSIC CLUBS

Legendary jazz club Akwarium has just been brought back to life, but for years the capital didn't have a jazz club to write home about until the emergence of 12on14 Jazz Club (http://12on14club.com) on 16 Noakowskiego street. It is a meeting place for jazz lovers with several weekly concerts featuring top national and international artists. Metro Jazz Bar & Bistro in the Metropol Hotel (www.hotelmetropol.com.pl) has concerts on Tue and Thu (8–10.30pm). You can also hear live jazz regularly at Klub Harenda (Krakowskie Przedmieście 4/6, entrance from Oboźna street) near the Warsaw University main campus. Hydrozagadka is a very popular music club in Praga, while Sen Pszczoły (www.senpszczoly.pl) is a versatile multi-purpose cultural center. Other popular venues with live music include Hybrydy (http://hybrydy.com.pl) and Stodoła (www.stodola.pl).

NIGHTLIFE

Under communism, Warsaw's streets used to empty around 9pm and only a few restaurants or bars stayed open later. Today it is normal to see crowds of people on a pub/club crawl at 1 or 2am on a weekday, not to mention weekends.

In summer, the riverbank is the place to be, with dozens of trendy bars and clubs blasting different music into the small hours. Some like Cud nad Wisłą (http://cudnadwisla.com), Plac Zabaw, BarKa or Hocki Klocki already enjoy a cult-like following. One word of warning though – Warsaw's night scene changes so rapidly it takes a well-informed local to tell you what places are up-and-coming and which ones have already begun to slide into oblivion.

CLUBBING

The main concentration of bars and nightclubs is in the city centre. Establishments around Piłsudski and Theatre square such as Opera club (www.operaclub.pl) cater for high-end clientele and follow a strict entry policy. More down-to-earth Mazowiecka street is simply a clubbers' paradise. A long list of places to dance your night away includes the veteran Organza (www.organza.pl), Room 13 (www.room13.pl) and Bank Club (http://bankclub.pl), the latter boasting a huge 1,200 sq m (12,916 sq ft) dance floor. Meanwhile, the exclusive XOXO (http://xoxoparty.pl) club located behind Sheraton Hotel features the best international DJs. The trendy Powiśle also has its fair share of clubs, as does Praga across the river.

Jazz in the Old Town

FESTIVALS

Warsaw's cultural festival calendar is brimming with interesting events taking place throughout the year, with a focus on music, film, culture and the arts.

MARCH/APRIL

Ludvig van Beethoven Easter Festival (www.beethoven.org.pl). Taking place a week before Easter, this top-notch classical music festival won the prestigious IFEA/Haass & Wilkerson Pinnacle Award in 2010 for the best arts event of the year. Symphonic and chamber concerts, performed by the world's best ensembles, soloists and directors, present Beethoven's music from different perspectives.

MAY

Millenium Docs Against Gravity Film Festival (http://docsag.pl). One of the biggest festivals of documentaries in Europe, it also features separate awards for the best films dedicated to environment protection and human rights.

JUNE/JULY

Warsaw Summer Jazz Days (www.adamiakjazz.pl) promote contemporary jazz and host the most innovative artists from different cultures and contrasting backgrounds. Highlights include a free concert at Plac Zamkowy (Royal Castle Square).

Mozart Festival. Warsaw Chamber Opera's (www.operakameralna.pl) flagship event for over 20 years, this features concerts held in venues including the Royal Castle and Łazienki's Palace.

Orange Festival. Held on the first weekend of June at the horse racing track in Służewiec, this eclectic festival brings together international and Polish artists representing different musical genres.

Międzynarodowy Festiwal Sztuka Ulicy (International Street Art Festival; http://sztukaulicy.pl). Dance, theatre, music and circus performances take place in city theatres, parks and public places, fostering cultural exchange in Europe. The festival attracts young people keen on avant garde and alternative art.

Piknik Naukowy (Science Picnic; www.pikniknaukowy.pl) held at PGE National Stadium in June: a feast of science for young and old with interesting experiments, workshops, hands-on displays and entertaining shows. It's the largest open air scientific event in Europe.

JULY–AUGUST

Jazz na Starówce (Jazz at the Old Town; July–August; www.jazznastarowce.pl).

Dancing at the Festival of Jewish Culture 'Singer's Warsaw'

Free jazz concerts featuring established international stars as well as newcomers. The performances take place every Saturday in July and August at the Old Town Square (7pm); people listen to the music with a beer or wine in the numerous outdoor gardens of nearby restaurants and cafés. The atmosphere is relaxed and artists are often eager to play something extra to please enthusiastic crowds.

Międzynarodowy Festiwal Chopin i jego Europa (International Music Festival Chopin and his Europe; http://pl.chopin.nifc.pl). Organised in August by the Fryderyk Chopin Institute. The concerts take place in the Polish Radio Concert Hall and National Opera, among others locations, with some pieces performed on historic instruments from the 19th century.

AUGUST–SEPTEMBER

Festival of Jewish Culture 'Singer's Warsaw' (late August/beginning of September; www.festiwalsingera.pl). Annual celebration of Jewish culture in all its forms that has been held since 2004. It takes place in the former Jewish quarter, mainly around Grzybowski Square and Próżna Street, and features klezmer concerts and cantor singing, but also lessons in Jewish paper-cutting and Hebrew calligraphy. Workshops allow people to try different kosher cuisine dishes. There are also films, workshops and seminars dedicated to every aspect of Jewish culture.

Warszawska Jesień (Warsaw Autumn International Festival of Contemporary Music; September; www.warszawska-jesien.art.pl). Founded in 1956 and an island of creative freedom for the entire Communist period, it was the only event of its kind in Central and Eastern Europe. Today, the festival features video projections and new technologies and has expanded to new venues across the city to woo the younger public. The concerts held through September present the best of new music and also take place in traditional halls such as the Warsaw Philharmonic, the Music Academy, and the city's theatres and churches.

OCTOBER

Warszawski Festiwal Filmowy (Warsaw Film Festival; October; www.wff.pl). Cinema buffs head for the capital to immerse themselves in a week-long film feast that showcases the best world productions. The programme is varied and aims to discover new trends in world cinema – it features independent films from all over the world, along with Hollywood blockbusters. There also workshops for film critics, journalists, directors and editors.

Jazz Jamboree (www.adamiakjazz.pl). Jazz Jamboree is one of the oldest jazz festivals in Europe (first held in 1958) but went into decline. It is now being revived by Mariusz Adamiak. The main concerts used to take place in the lavish Sala Kongresowa (now under renovation), which has seen performances by the greatest jazz stars, including Miles Davis, Chick Corea and Paco de Lucia.

Adoption of the Polish Constitution on 3 May 1791

HISTORY: KEY DATES

Warsaw, which has been Poland's capital for 400 years, encapsulates the country's turbulent history like no other place. It's history is reflected today in the city's diverse architecture and atmosphere.

MIDDLE AGES

10th century	Bródno is the earliest fortified settlement within Warsaw borders.
1313	The earliest mention of Warsaw in historical records.
1339	A trial involving Poland and the Teutonic Knights takes place in the church of St John.

GLORY AND WAR

1526	Mazovia is integrated with the Kingdom of Poland.
1569	The beginnings of modem Warsaw. The city is chosen as the location for the parliament of the Polish-Lithuanian Commonwealth.
1573	The first Royal Election in Poland.
1596	The royal court of Zygmunt III moves from Kraków to Warsaw.
1655	Warsaw's development is interrupted by the Swedish invasion.
1697	Saxon era begins with the election of August II Mocny of Saxony.
1700	Outbreak of the Northern War with Sweden; catastrophic consequences for Poland.
1713	Reconstruction of the city under supervision of the Saxon Bauamt.
1764	Stanisław August Poniatowski, Poland's last king, is elected.

UNDER FOREIGN RULE

1772	The First Partition of Poland.
1791	Enactment of 3 May Constitution – only the world's second.
1793	The Second Partition of Poland.
1794	Outbreak of the Kościuszko Uprising.
1795	The Third Partition of Poland and the demise of the Commonwealth. Warsaw becomes part of Prussia.

The ruins of the Old Town in Warsaw after the war, 1945

1807	Establishment of the Napoleonic Duchy of Warsaw.
1815	Warsaw becomes capital of the Congress Kingdom of Poland.
1830	November Uprising, ending in defeat and Russian reprisals.
1863	January Uprising.
1915	After the outbreak of World War I, the Russian authorities and army abandon Warsaw.

INDEPENDENCE AND WORLD WAR II

1918	On 11 November, Poland regains independence.
1920	On the outskirts of Warsaw, Józef Piłsudski defeats the Red Army.
1939	Outbreak of World War II. Warsaw capitulates after several weeks of resistance.
1943	The Jewish Ghetto Uprising.
1944	The Warsaw Uprising, a national revolt against German occupation, takes place from August to October; the city is deliberately destroyed by German soldiers.
1945	Russian and Polish soldiers enter the ruined left bank of Warsaw.

COMMUNISM AND BEYOND

1956	The beginnings of the 'thaw' and the assumption of power by Władysław Gomułka.
1968	Student demonstrations.
1980	Registration of the Solidarity Trade Union in Warsaw.
1981	Martial law is declared on 13 December.
1989	'Round Table' talks and parliamentary elections end in defeat for the communists.
1995	The first metro line opens in the capital.

21ST CENTURY

2004	Poland joins the European Union.
2010	95 people including President Lech Kaczyński die when the presidential plane crashes in Russia.
2012	Poland joint-hosts the Euro 2012 football championships.
2016	A NATO summit is held at the National Stadium.
2018	Municipal elections.

BEST ROUTES

Sigismund's Column and the Royal Castle

OLD TOWN

Hands down the most popular and famous part of Warsaw, the Old Town encapsulates the city's indomitable spirit and stormy history. This route wends its way through quaint narrow streets to the beautifully restored market square.

DISTANCE: 1.5km (1 mile)
TIME: Half a day, especially if you visit museums
START: Sigismund's Column
END: Barbican
POINTS TO NOTE: Avoid doing this route on Monday as most museums are closed. You can easily combine this walk with Route 2 or Route 3. Wear comfortable shoes (high heels are not recommended) to pound the cobbles.

A Unesco World Heritage Site, the Old Town attracts crowds of tourists. It occupies a relatively small area that can be toured in less than an hour, but if you want to explore the Royal Castle with its lavish interiors and interesting collection of paintings or learn more about town's history at the renovated Museum of Warsaw, you will need more than that.

SIGISMUND'S COLUMN

Overlooking the Castle Square (Plac Zamkowy) and usually surrounded by people, the 22-metre (72ft) high **Sigismund's Column ❶** (Kolumna Zygmunta) is topped with a figure of the king Sigismund III Vasa armed with a sword (a symbol of knighthood), and a cross (reflecting his counter-reformatory stance). Designed by Italian architect Agostino Locci (the elder), it was unveiled in 1644. The monument's base of the monument was changed several times and the present granite shaft had two predecessors that now lie next to the Royal Castle. The column was destroyed by the Germans in 1944 and reconstructed two years later with the original figure.

THE ROYAL CASTLE

Opposite Sigismund's Column is the elegant silhouette of the **Royal Castle ❷** (Zamek Królewski, Pl. Zamkowy 4, www.zamek-krolewski.pl; Royal Apartments and Grand Apartments Oct–Apr Tue–Sat 10am–4pm, Sun 11am–4pm, May–Sep Mon–Wed and Fri–Sat 10am–6pm, Thu until 8pm, Sun 11am–6pm; free on Sun, but the route is shorter) dominating the square (see box).

The Castle's Old Audience Chamber

The Tin-Roofed Palace and Kubicki Arcades

Adjoining the royal castle is **The Tin-Roofed Palace** (Pałac Pod Blachą; same hours). This Baroque palace has a collection of rugs and carpets, with rare examples from Persia and Turkey, and the world's largest collection of Caucasian rugs. The castle's gardens, by the old riverbed, contain the beautifully restored **Kubicki Arcades** (Arkady Kubickiego; close one hour later), built from 1818 to 1821. The arcades are used now as an exhibition and cultural centre.

ST JOHN'S CATHEDRAL

Back on the Castle Square, take Świętojańska street and walk to **St John's Cathedral** ❸ (Katedra Św Jana Chrzciciela; Świętojańska 8; www.katedra.mkw.pl; daily; crypt: Mon–Sat 10am–5pm, Sun 3–5pm). Warsaw's oldest church, and the largest in the Old Town, the cathedral was rebuilt after World War II in the original 14th-century style known as Vistulan Gothic, defined by an austere but spiritual simplicity. The crypt contains tombs of various Mazovian dukes and some of Poland's most renowned leaders and artists, including Nobel Prize-winning novelist Henryk Sienkiewicz (1846–1916), author of *Quo Vadis*. A side altar contains the sarcophagus of Poland's former primate, Cardinal Stefan Wyszyński, a mentor of the Pope John Paul II.

Next to St. John's Cathedral is the **Jesuit Church** (Kościół Jezuitów), one of the

The Royal Castle

A castle was first established on its current location in the 13th century as the residence of the Mazovian dukes. From the end of the 16th century it became the royal residence, as well as the seat of parliament. In 1791 the 3rd of May Constitution was drawn up here, the first of its kind in Europe. Between the two World Wars, the castle was the president's official residence. The Nazis' total destruction of the castle extended to drilling thousands of holes in the foundations for sticks of dynamite (a few holes can still be seen in the crypt). The castle was rebuilt thanks to private subscriptions raised in Poland and from émigré Poles around the world. Opened in 1984, the surviving architectural fragments, including Baroque, Gothic and rococo styles, were incorporated into a recreation of the 17th-century façade. The interiors are largely 18th-century. The pillared and gilded ballroom is in contrast to the mausoleum-like character of the Marble Room, or the Picture Gallery devoted to views of Warsaw painted by Bernardo Bellotto (known as Canaletto in Poland). In the former chapel is an urn containing the heart of the Polish hero Tadeusz Kościuszko (1746–1817) who led Polish troops against the Russians in a bid for freedom during the partitions, and was also a hero of the American War of Independence.

St John's Cathedral

finest examples of the mannerist style in the capital. Note the bronze doors which were made by the late world-famous Polish sculptor Igor Mitoraj in 2009. They represent the scene of annunciation to the Blessed Virgin Mary whose representation was inspired by the classic sculpture of the Venus de Milo.

Piwna street

At this stage you may want to refuel at the small restaurant **Zapiecek**, see ❶, known for its excellent *pierogi* and located just opposite the cathedral. You can take a short stroll there to see the undulating late-baroque façade of the **Franciscan Nuns' Church of St Martin** (Kościół Franciszkanek św. Marcina). The house at no. 6 has a flock of pigeons above its portal; this stone sculpture dating from 1952–53 commemorates the 'Pigeon Fancier' ('*Gołębiarka*') – an old woman who could often be seen in the ruins just after the war, feeding the birds. Retrace your steps to Świętojańska and turn into Dziekania passing through the gate in the cathedral's bell-tower.

DZIEKANIA

Embedded in the cathedral wall are the caterpillar tracks from a German minelayer, deployed by the Germans during the Warsaw Uprising to destroy a barricade. More than 300 people died in an explosion of one of those devices on 13th August 1944. On the right, you will find the **Warsaw Archdiocese Museum** ❹

(Muzeum Archidiecezji Warszawskiej; Dziekania 1, http://maw.art.pl; Tue–Fri noon–6pm, Sat–Sun noon–4pm).

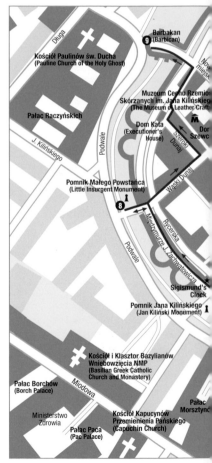

Piwna street

Boasting a collection of canonicals, jewellery and sculpture, its biggest attraction are woodcuts by Albrecht Dürer, an interesting collection of Polish paintings, including works by Jan Matejko, Stanisław Wyspiański, Józef Pankiewicz

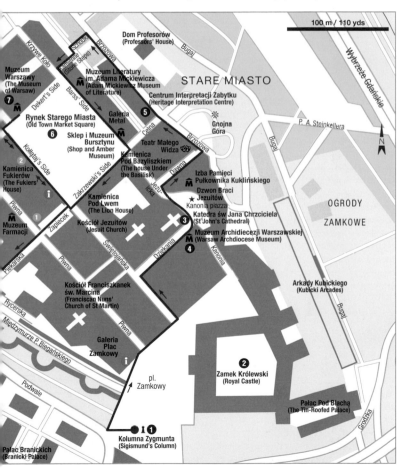

Dom Profesorów
(Professors' House)

Schody
Brzozowa

Kamienne
Schody
(Stone Steps)

Muzeum
Warszawy
(The Museum
of Warsaw)
7

Muzeum Literatury
im. Adama Mickiewicza
(Adam Mickiewicz Museum
of Literature)

Dekert's Side

Bars' Side

STARE MIASTO

Bugaj

Wybrzeże Gdańskie

Galeria
Metal

Centrum Interpretacji Zabytku
(Heritage Interpretation Centre)

5

Celna

Gnojna
Góra

P. A. Steinkellera

Rynek Starego Miasta
(Old Town Market Square)
6

Sklep i Muzeum
Bursztynu
(Shop and Amber
Museum)

Teatr Małego
Widza

Kołłątaj's Side

Kamienica
Pod Bazyliszkiem
(The house Under
the Basilisk)

Brzozowa

Kamienica
Fukierów
(The Fukiers'
House)
2

Zakrzewski's Side

Dawna

Izba Pamięci
Pułkownika Kuklińskiego

Piwna

Kamienica
Pod Lwem
(The Lion House)

Icka

Jezu

Dzwon Braci
Jezuitów
★
Kanonia piazza

OGRODY

Muzeum
Farmaci
M

Zapiecek

1

Kościół Jezuitów
(Jesuit Church)

3
Katedra św Jana Chrzciciela
(St John's Cathedral)

Muzeum Archidiecezji Warszawskiej
(Warsaw Archdiocese Museum)
4

ZAMKOWE

Piekarska

Świętojańska

Dziekania

Kanonia

Kościół Franciszkanek
św. Marcina
(Franciscan Nuns'
Church of St Martin)

Rycerska

Międzymurze P. Biegańskiego

Piwna

Arkady Kubickiego
(Kubicki Arcades)

Bugaj

Podwale

Galeria
Plac
Zamkowy

pl.
Zamkowy

2
Zamek Królewski
(Royal Castle)

Pałac Pod Blachą
(The Tin-Roofed Palace)

Grodzka

1
Kolumna Zygmunta
(Sigismund's Column)

Pałac Branickich
(Branicki Palace)

100 m / 110 yds

Kanonia piazza's bell

and Jacek Malczewski, and Polish independent art from the 1980s, represented by artists who left communist Poland such as Józef Czapski.

KANONIA PIAZZA

The exit of Dziekania is closed by a covered walkway, which once linked the Royal Castle with the cathedral. It was built after a failed assassination attempt on Zygmunt III Vasa in 1620. Polish monarchs would enter the cathedral via the walkway. Passing through the gate, you reach the small Kanonia square, which until 1790 served as a cemetery. In the middle stands a beautiful bell made by Daniel Tym (who also cast Sigismund III Vasa's monument on the column) dating from 1646; it has never actually sounded (a design error). Take a look at the house at no. 20/22, the narrowest in Poland, with a façade that is less than 2 metres (79in) wide. This way, the shrewd owner avoided higher taxes.

JEZUICKA AND DAWNA

Enter Jezuicka street. On the wall, next to the first gate on the left, you will find an embedded plaque in memory of Grzegorz Przemyk, a 19-year old student, son of an opposition member and promising young poet, who was beaten to death in 1983 by three members of the communist police at the police station that used to be located at Jezuicka 1/3. Then turn right into Dawna street. This back street

exudes a romantic charm and has frequently been used as a set by Polish filmmakers. Slightly further on, it opens out onto Brzozowa street and a broad terrace affording a beautiful view of the Vistula. Unveiled in 1908, a sculpture of a man lifting a huge stone was made by the Polish artist Stanisław Czarnowski.

BRZOZOWA STREET

Brzozowa is a picturesque street laid out on an embankment at the foot of the city walls. It was once called 'Between the Granaries' (Między Spichlerzami), on account of the storehouses that faced the river here. Continue on Brzozowa to reach the **Heritage Interpretation Centre** ❺ (Centrum Interpretacji Zabytku; ul. Brzozowa 11/13; http://ciz.muzeum warszawy.pl, Tue–Sun 10am–7pm; free on Thu) a branch of the Museum of Warsaw documenting the history of the Old Town's reconstruction after World War II.

Further down Brzozowa, on your right-hand side you will see another plaque embedded in the wall. The **Professors' House** (Dom Profesorów; located behind the wall across the stone bridge) a former granary and later residence of Warsaw University's professors, which was a Polish stronghold that withheld all German attacks during the Warsaw Uprising.

KAMIENNE SCHODKI

Following Brzozowa, you eventually reach the picturesque **Stone Steps** (Kamienne

Heritage Interpretation Centre *Nightlife in the Old Town Market Square*

Schodki). This steepest street in Warsaw (a flight of steep stairs in fact) is full of charm; it has been a favourite open-air location for photographers and artists for two centuries. The stairs lead to Old Town's Market Square.

Old Town Market Square

The **Old Town Market Square ❻** (Rynek Starego Miasta), laid out at the turn of the 13th century, is always bustling with people visiting the square's numerous cafés, bars and restaurants, while street-traders and artists ply their wares outside the galleries and shops. A constant stream of tourists fills the place at all hours. In summer the square is covered with café tables, while horse-drawn carriages clip-clop from here to the Old Town (closed to traffic). Free jazz concerts are organised here every Saturday in July and August (see page 24).

Beautifully recreated burghers' houses, dating from the 15th and 16th centuries, line the square and each side is named after a member of the four-year Sejm that passed the 3 May Constitution in 1791: Ignacy Zakrzewski (south side), Franciszek Barss (east side), Jan Dekert (north side) and Hugo Kołłątaj (west side).

Museum of Warsaw

The **Museum of Warsaw ❼** (Muzeum Warszawy; Rynek Starego Miasta 28–42; http://muzeumwarszawy.pl; Tue–Sun 10am–7pm) occupies the entire length of the Dekert side. The house at no. 36 is decorated with an African head, a gilded

portal and sgraffito. The house (1632) is a reminder of the prosperity of the Commonwealth before the catastrophic Swedish invasion of the mid-17th century. Featuring a Renaissance portal, it is one of three burghers' houses which were linked behind their façades to accommodate the main seat of the museum. Over the years, it has accumulated over 300,000 exhibits including clocks, furniture, sculptures, photographs, panoramas and pieces of clothing as well as jewellery and weapons, with the oldest object dating back to the 14th century. Having reopened in 2017 after two years of intensive renovation, there is a permanent exhibition called **The Things of Warsaw** comprising nearly 7,500 objects, arranged across 21 rooms. A popular observation point on the roof of one of the townhouses offers amazing views over the Old Town.

Barss side (east)

Leaving the museum, take a left, passing the Kamienne Schodki restaurant – famous for its Polish style duck – to reach the **Adam Mickiewicz Museum of Literature** (Muzeum Literatury im. Adama Mickiewicza; Mon, Tue and Fri 10am–4pm, Wed–Thu 11am–6pm, Sun 11am–5pm) dedicated to the greatest Polish romantic poet. The museum also provides insights into the life and work of other Polish writers.

Further on is a jewellery shop, **Galeria Metal** (at no. 8) selling the works of the Polish designer Marcin Zaremski (http://zaremski.pl) as well as the **Shop**

View over the square towards the Museum of Warsaw

and **Amber Museum** (at no.4/6; www. muzeumbursztynu.com), which offers jewellery and souvenirs made of amber.

Zakrzewski side (south)

The most famous landmark on the south side of the square is the **Under the Basilisk** (Pod Bazyliszkiem) house, located at no. 5, with Bazyliszek restaurant on the ground floor, and renowned for its Gothic cellars. Legend has it that once they were full of treasures guarded by a mythical monster, the Basilisk, whose gaze would turn to stone anyone brave enough to venture inside. However, a shrewd tailor defeated the beast by hiding himself behind a mirror. One look was enough for the Basilisk to petrify himself. The corner building at no. 13 is **the Lion House** (Kamienica Pod Lwem); its façade, painted in 1928–9, is an excellent example of Polish Art Deco.

Kołłątaj side (west)

The west side of the square includes a post office (in the house at the corner) and the Tourist Office at no. 19 (daily 9am–6pm). Further on at no. 27 is the **Fukiers' House** (Kamienica Fukierów), housing the famous restaurant **U Fukiera**, see ②, owned by Polish chief and celebrity Magda Gessler. At no. 31 is the beautiful **Plumhoff House** (Kamienica Plumhoffowska), dating from before 1466. The centrally located bronze **mermaid fountain** by Konstanty Hegel dates back to the 19th century and is a favourite of children on hot days.

ZAPIECEK AND PIEKARSKA STREET

Return to the post office and turn into the wide, square-like Zapiecek street. Continue down on Piekarska street, past Portretowa Restaurant. Few steps further on your left looms a huge **Jan Kiliński Monument** (Pomnik Jana Kilińskiego), with a bronze figure of Warsaw's cobbler Jan Kiliński, hero of the 1794 Kościuszko Uprising. During World War II, the figure was stealthily hidden by the Germans in the vaults of the National Museum. However, the secret was soon revealed – only a few days later, boy scouts daubed the museum's wall with graffiti saying 'People of Warsaw, I am here, Jan Kiliński'.

Little Insurgent Monument

From the monument, take the alley to the right (not Rycerska street!) leading between two red-brick defensive walls, and head north. The double ring of walls strengthened with towers and bastions was built between the 14th–17th centuries. Later, when they ceased to play a defensive role, the walls disappeared, but after World War II, extensive sections were restored.

Follow the right-bending alley to the Wąski Dunaj street (until the white building housing Bar and Books pub). From here, make a short detour. Turn left to the zebra crossing, cross the street, and go the cobbled alley along the ramparts. After few meters, you will see the **Little Insurgent Monument** ❽ (Pomnik

Little Insurgent Monument

Małego Powstańca) on your right, dedicated to all children who fought and died during the Warsaw Uprising (adolescent boys were used as runners delivering orders between the units). Designed in 1949, but not unveiled until 1983, the small monument became a powerful symbol of the Warsaw Uprising for many years, as the communist authorities refused to properly commemorate the fallen fighters. Retrace your steps to the zebra crossing and turn left into Wąski Dunaj towards the Old Town's centre.

WĄSKI DUNAJ, SZEROKI DUNAJ

Walk up Wąski Dunaj and then turn right into Szeroki Dunaj street, where people bought flowers and vegetables in the 19th century. During the reconstruction of the Old Town, stories about market traders with baskets of fish and piles of fruit were painted onto the façades of the houses on both streets.

Go past the **Museum of Leather Crafts** (Muzeum Cechu Rzemiosł Skórzanych im. Jana Kilińskiego; www.cech janakilinskiego.waw.pl; Thu–Sat 10am–3pm, free) to reach the former **Executioner's House** (Dom Kata) at the end of Szeroki Dunaj. Go through the gate to enter the alley between the ramparts. Turn right to the Barbican.

THE BARBICAN

A semi-circular fortified outpost, the **Barbican ❾** (Barbakan), formed part of the original 16th century defensive fortifications. Nearly completely destroyed in the war, it was restored in the 1950s according to 17th-century engravings. Nowadays, it's an artists' domain, where creatives offer their works to tourists.

From the Barbican, you could continue and follow Route 2, or head back to the Old Town's Market Square.

Food and drink

❶ ZAPIECEK

Świętojańska 13; tel. 022 635 61 09; www.zapiecek.eu; daily 11am–11pm; €€
Although it's a chain of restaurants, the picrogi here are good quality and served in a traditional way with butter, sour cream, cranberry or small fried pieces of onion or bacon. There are also sweet versions. Friendly waitresses wear folk costumes.

❷ U FUKIERA

Rynek Starego Miasta 27; tel. 022 831-10-13; http://ufukiera.pl; daily noon–midnight; €€€€
Owned by local celebrity restaurateur Magda Gessler, U Fukiera is one of the oldest restaurants in Warsaw (going back to the 16th century) and also one of the priciest on the market square. It serves Warsaw staples such as herring, tripe soup and roasted duck, plus international fare. The interior recalls a Polish country estate with paintings on the walls, vintage hutches and buckets of flowers.

Freta street life

NEW TOWN AND BEYOND

Neighbour to the much hyped Starówka, the New Town and its surroundings have plenty to offer for inquisitive explorers, be it historic buildings, half-forgotten narrow alleyways, museums or high-tech entertainment.

DISTANCE: 2.3km (1.4 miles)
TIME: Three hours
START: Barbican
END: Krakowskie Przedmieście
POINTS TO NOTE: The route is a continuation of the Route 1 and can be connected to Route 3 as well. On Mon, Tue or Sat you will not be able to visit all the museums. Shows at the fountain park began on summer weekends at 9 or 9.30pm.

Adjacent to the Old Town, the New Town is much more compact and can be easily explored on foot in an hour, unless you intend to visit the museums.

FRETA

Passing through the **Barbican**'s brick gate ❶ (see page 37), follow Nowomiejska (that soon becomes Freta) to enter the New Town, which emerged at the turn of the 14th century and developed as a wholly separate municipal entity from the Old Town. In summer, the New Town fills up with tourists, attracted by the numerous pavement cafes and convivial atmosphere. One such is the milk bar at the corner of the picturesque Mostowa street, while wonderful coffee smells draw you to the Pożegnanie z Afryką cafe at Nos 4-6.

Each year, in August, pilgrimages to the Jasna Góra monastery in southern Poland depart from the baroque **Pauline Church of the Holy Ghost** (Kościół Paulinów św. Ducha) at the corner of Długa street. A place full of curiosities is the **Dominican Church of St Hyacinth** (Kościół Dominikanów św. Jacka), situated further up the street, on the other side. Its interior is set well below street level, as the church was built on the steep Vistula bank.

MARIE SKŁODOWSKA-CURIE MUSEUM

Just behind the church, at No 16, is the birthplace of Marie Skłodowska-Curie, twice winner of the Nobel prize (see box). The recently renovated house is now the **Marie Skłodowska-Curie Museum** ❷

Facade of the Maria Skłodowska-Curie Museum

(Muzeum Marii Skłodowskiej-Curie; http://muzeum-msc.pl; Tue–Sat Sep–May 10am–4.30pm, Jun–Aug 10am–7pm) showcasing research documents, tools and personal items related to the world-famous scientist, as well the

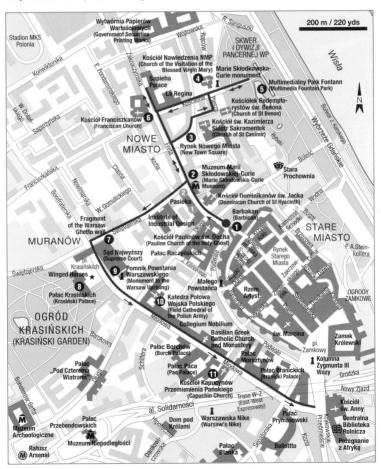

The New Town Square

reconstruction of her Parisian laboratory and the history of Polish chemistry.

Marie Curie

Born Maria Skłodowska on New Town's Freta street in Russian-ruled Warsaw, Marie Curie showed great passion for knowledge from her early years, learning to read young and to speak five foreign languages fluently. However, her family struggled financially, and Marie lost her mother when she was ten. As Russian authorities would not allow women to attend university, she left for Paris where she studied physics, chemistry and mathematics. There she also met her future husband – the talented physician Pierre Curie. In 1903 Marie became the first woman to receive a Nobel Prize in physics, co-shared with Pierre, for discovering radioactivity. Nearly a decade later, having overcome the sudden death of her much-loved husband, she would became the first scientist (and the only woman to date) to be awarded a second Nobel Prize (in chemistry) for discovering radium and polonium. Marie was a trailblazer in so many ways: she was the first woman-professor at Sorbonne University, one of the first women to hold a driving license and the first scientist to hold celebrity status, which she hated. As her long-time friend Albert Einstein once said: 'Marie Curie is of all celebrated beings, the only one whom fame has not corrupted'.

Across the street, **Pod Samsonem**, see ❶, is a nice place for lunch. Two bas-reliefs under balconies represent Samson slaying the lion and Delilah cutting off Samson's hair. Two houses further up, on the same side of the street, Pasieka restaurant is known for its great selection of traditional Polish meads. Another sweet treat awaits at no. 13/15 where the **Wedel chocolate lounge**, see ❷, boasts a centrally located fountain.

NEW TOWN SQUARE

From Freta you enter the **New Town Square** ❸ (Rynek Nowego Miasta), whose houses were rebuilt after the war in a late 18th-century style. At its centre is the 19th-century well. Compared with the crowded Old Town Square, its New Town counterpart is refreshingly peaceful. Above its eastern side rises the green dome of the **Church of St Casimir** (Kościół św. Kazimierza Sióstr Sakramentek), built in 1688–92 by King Jan III Sobieski and his wife, Queen Marysieńka.

Running east off the New Town Square is Piesza, a small passageway with a vista of the tiny **Church of St Benon** (Kościółek Redemptorystów św. Benona). The interior of the church is surprisingly modern, although it incorporates some expressive old sculptures. Soon you will reach the Gothic **Church of the Visitation of the Blessed Virgin Mary** ❹ (Kościół Nawiedzenia NMP), the oldest place of worship in the New Town,

Light show at the Multimedia Fountain Park

and founded at the beginning of the 15th century by Anna, Duchess of Mazovia. The church you see today is a reconstruction, but the rebuilding project after World War II involved the use of methods similar to those practised in the Middle Ages. After leaving the church, stop for a few moments at the exit of Kościelna street to admire the beautiful panorama of the Vistula valley, with the Old Town perched high on a bluff. Overlooking the river stands the **Marie Skłodowska-Curie monument**. The bronze figure of the scientist holds a model of Polonium, which she discovered. A gift from the Association of Legion of Honor's Members and a symbol of Polish-French friendship, it was unveiled by French President François Hollande and his Polish counterpart Bronisław Komorowski in 2014 on the 80th anniversary of the scientist's death. It is said, it stands in a place young Maria used to frequent to look at the river.

FOUNTAIN PARK

A flight of wooden stairs right to the monument lead to the **Multimedia Fountain Park ❺** (www.parkfontann. pl), a complex of four fountains where highly popular, 30-minute light, water and sound shows are held every Friday and Saturday from May to September (at 9 or 9.30pm).

Back on Kościelna, follow the street past the elegant La Regina Hotel and turn right into Zakroczymska street to see the **Franciscan Church ❻** (Kościół Franciszkanów) standing on the corner of Franciszkańska street. The church's neo-Classical façade, with two towers in the form of obelisks, conceals a baroque interior, whose main point of interest is a glass coffin containing the holy relics of the Roman martyr St Vitalis, which were given to the Franciscans by Pope Benedict XIV in 1754.

ZAKROCZYMSKA STREET TO ŚWIĘTOJERSKA

Continue on Zakroczymska until, on the right-hand side (no. 6), you will find the rococo façade of the **Sapieha Palace** (Pałac Sapiehów), dating from 1731–46, now a school. Just behind the palace, to the right, is a large complex of modernist buildings from the 1920s, among which is the **Government Securities Printing Works** (Wytwórnia Papierów Wartościowych).

From here, return to the Franciscan church. On the wall of Franciszkańska street look for a plaque indicating the eastern edge of the northern boundary of the Warsaw Ghetto. Take Freta toward the Old Town, passing cafés and restaurants as well as the New Town square on your way. Turn right onto Świętojerska street.

On your right-hand side, at no. 5/7, is a building of the **Institute of Industrial Design** (Instytut Wzornictwa Przemysłowego; www.iwp.com.pl) dedicated to promoting ergonomic design. On the corner of Nowiniarska street, do not miss the

Krasiński Palace

only remaining fragment of the **Warsaw Ghetto wall** embedded in the pavement. Continue along Świętojerska to the Krasiński Square (Plac Krasińskich).

KRASIŃSKI SQUARE

Two huge sections of the square are now occupied by the **Supreme Court** (Sąd Najwyższy; www.sn.pl). The court building is flanked by massive green columns (so called 'law columns') with quotes taken from Roman law. Across the street, the recently renovated **Krasiński Palace** ❽ (Pałac Krasińskich), completed in 1683 for the voivode (provincial governor) of Płock Jan Dobrogost Krasiński, is the most beautiful example of mature Roman baroque in Warsaw. The façades are noteworthy, particularly the bas-reliefs. Burnt down in 1944, the palace was rebuilt again after the war. It now houses a library including valuable manuscripts and old prints from the National Library collection as well as an archive of Polish jazz, documenting the history of this musical genre in Poland. Behind the palace is the beautiful **Krasiński Garden** (Ogród Krasińskich).

Opposite the palace, next to the Supreme Court seat, is the dramatic **Monument to the Warsaw Uprising** ❾ (Pomnik Powstania Warszawskiego). Unveiled in 1989, it consists of two sections: the main one shows a group of Polish fighters trying to flee from the crumbling building while a smaller one features soldiers descending into the city sewers, a reference to the dramatic escape from the besieged Old Town during the Warsaw Uprising. Dynamism and movement, euphoria and drama are all captured in bronze and granite. In 1994, German President Roman Herzog made history laying flowers at the monument and extending an apology to the Polish people for crimes committed by the Germans during World War II.

FIELD CATHEDRAL OF THE POLISH ARMY

On the opposite side of Długa (at numbers 13–15) rise the twin towers of a 17th-century former church, which now serves as the **Field Cathedral of the Polish Army** ❿ (Katedra Polowa Wojska Polskiego). A huge anchor and plane propeller guard the entrance to the church. Inside are numerous plaques commemorating Polish soldiers fighting on all fronts of World War II and a somber **Katyń Chapel** (Kaplica Katyńska) devoted to the over 21,000 Polish prisoners (officers, policemen and civilians) who were murdered in Katyń forest, Miednoje and Charków in spring 1940 by the Soviet secret police (NKVD) under Stalin's orders. The marble altar of the chapel is decorated with the Madonna's icon with an aureole made of buttons removed from the uniforms of soldiers found in the mass graves. Names of the 15,000 Poles murdered there are engraved on side walls. Exit the church and turn into Miodowa street.

Warsaw Uprising monument   *Branicki Palace*

MIODOWA

Continue along Miodowa, whose name ('Honey Street') derives from the confectioners and pastry chefs who once lived here. The neo-Classical building at no. 22–4 used to belong to the **Collegium Nobilium**, the famous 18th-century academy for young nobles, established by Father Stanisław Konarski. Behind, is the neo-Classical facade of the **Basilian Greek Catholic Church and Monastery** (Kościół i Klasztor Bazylianów Wniebowzięcia NMP). The former **Borch Palace** (Pałac Borchów) across the street (no. 17) was the residence of the Primate of Poland until 2007. Beautiful eclectic interiors distinguish the **Pac Palace** (Pałac Paca) at no. 15, which is also remarkable for its concave gateway topped by a neo-Classical frieze; today it serves as the site of the Ministry of Health. Slightly further on, at No 13, is the **Capuchin Church** ⑪ (Kościół Kapucynów Przemienienia Pańskiego). This baroque structure, dating from 1683–92, is rather modest, and the altars, in keeping with the Capuchin rule, are devoid of gilding. The remains of several famous people are found here, most notably King Jan III Sobieski, whose heart is kept in an urn inside the royal chapel.

Just beyond the church emerges the East-West Expressway (Trasa W–Z), begun when Warsaw was still in ruins and completed in 1949. Look right to see a gigantic monument (21 metres/69ft high) of the **Warsaw's Nike** (Warszawska Nike) in the distance, one of the city's symbols that shows a figure of a rising woman holding a sword over her head.

Continue walking on Miodowa past the façade of the 18th- and 19th-century **Branicki Palace** (Pałac Branickich), and yet another baroque palace (no.5) which once belonged to the bishops of Cracow. A sharp bent to the right, where Krakowskie Przedmieście street starts, marks the end of this tour.

AROUND KRAKOWSKIE PRZEDMIEŚCIE

This route allows you to explore the most prestigious thoroughfare of the capital, which boasts elegant palaces, impressive churches, the president's seat and luxurious hotels.

DISTANCE: 3.3km (2 miles)
TIME: Two hours, more if you visit museums
START/END: Church of St Anne
POINTS TO NOTE: the best day for this route is Thursday, when museums are free. If in a hurry, it can be combined with Route 4 – after Krakowskie Przedmieście, continue on Nowy Świat. It's also easy to combine with Route 1 and Route 7.

Krakowskie Przedmieście street marks the beginning (or the end) of the so-called Royal Route (Trakt Królewski) linking the Old Town with Wilanów Palace. It is a favourite stroll for Varsovians and a good way to see numerous historic sites with almost no visual interference from modern buildings. Until the Partitions of Poland in the late 18th century, Krakowskie Przedmieście was Warsaw's main thoroughfare; along it, Poland's newly elected kings would make their triumphant entry to the city. Today, the street is lined with baroque churches and monasteries, as well as the Polish aristocracy's houses and palaces, which were all rebuilt after being destroyed in World War II.

A NEW LOOK

In 2008 Krakowskie Przedmieście underwent a dramatic makeover. The pavements were expanded to create a wide pedestrianised area and a special, yellowish granite was imported from China to make the street look just like Canaletto's paintings. You can listen to Chopin's music and learn about his life and times at the 'Chopin benches' spread across the town; a few of them are located at Krakowskie Przedmieście. Made of cast iron and polished black stone, they are strategically located in places linked to the great Polish pianist and composer. When you press a button, you can hear a 30-second long piece of Chopin's music. You can also gains access to more Chopin music, facts and figures related to his life and work by sending a code to the instructed number.

Crowds on Krakowskie Przedmieście

CHURCH OF ST ANNE

Begin the tour by visiting the magnificent **Church of St Anne** ❶ (Kościół św. Anny). Remodelled in the 18th century and reconstructed after World War II, it is one of Warsaw's most treasured monuments. The nave is decorated with superb *trompe-l'oeil* murals from the 18th century, depicting scenes from the life of St Anne. In the adjoining monastery cloisters, the high point is the beautiful late-Gothic vaulting. You can climb 150 stone stairs to the **observation deck** (www.taraswidokowy.pl; Krakowskie Przedmieście 68; May–Oct

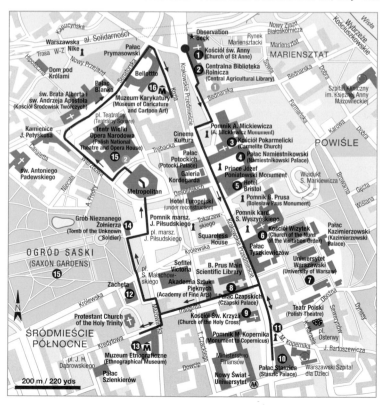

View from the tower at the Church of St Anne

Mon–Fri 10am–9pm, Sat–Sun 11am–10pm, Oct–May closes at 6pm) of the church's bell tower for breath-taking views of the Castle Square, the Vistula and Krakowskie Przedmieście. The church is a centre of Academic Ministry and a popular wedding place.

Next to St. Anne's Church at no.66 is the **Central Agricultural Library** ❷ (Centralna Biblioteka Rolnicza) with a characteristic classicist colonnade. Originally built in mid-15th century as a Bernardine monastery, it was rebuilt several times and once served as a guards' house for Prussian, French and Polish troops, at the turn of 18th to 19th century. A century later it housed the Museum of Industry and Agriculture, and was a venue of the clandestine Flying University. It was here that young Marie Skłodowska (later Curie) conducted her first chemical experiments. A commemorative plaque, with a hole from the German bullet fired during the 1944 Uprising, still hangs on the building's façade.

ADAM MICKIEWICZ MONUMENT

Continue on the right side of Krakowskie Przedmieście, past the corner of **Bednarska**. At this point, you can decide to go all the way down Bednarska to the Powiśle (see Route 7). Famous **Pierogarnia**, see ❶, on the left-side of the street, is known for its excellent selection of *pierogi* (dumplings).

At the far end of a green stretch to your right stands the **Adam Mickiewicz Monument** (Pomnik Adama Mickiewicza), unveiled in 1898 on the occasion of the 100th birth anniversary of Poland's foremost Romantic poet. In summer, the green square in the middle often hosts concerts and other cultural events. Close by is the former **Carmelite Church** ❸ (Kościół Pokarmelicki), dating from 1661–82, whose interior is full of sumptuous baroque altars; the stone façade of 1782 is one of the earliest examples of neo-Classicism in Poland. Across the street is the cinema **Kultura** (www.restauracjakultura.com.pl) which luckily survived a difficult democratic transformation. Nowadays, having been renovated and modernized, it is one of the best arthouse cinemas in Poland.

Further on, on the right-hand side, you pass the baroque **Potocki Palace** (Pałac Potockich) at no. 15, once a headquarter of Nikolay Novosiltsev – the notorious head of the tsar's secret police and de facto ruler of the Congress Kingdom of Poland between 1815–30. Today this glamorous palace hosts the Ministry of Culture and National Heritage. Established in 1956, a prestigious **Galeria Kordegarda** (www.kordegarda.org) art gallery is located in the palace's former watchtower.

PRESIDENTIAL PALACE

On the left at Nos 48–50 stands the **Namiestnikowski Palace** ❹ (Pałac

The Presidential Palace

Namiestnikowski), also known as the Presidential Palace. The latter residence was built in the 17th century for the Grand Hetman (commander-in-chief) Stanisław Koniecpolski who, as well as being a first-rate military leader, was famous for his amorous involvements with women.

In 1955, the Warsaw Pact was signed here, and in 1989 the palace provided the setting for the historic Round Table talks between the communist government and the Solidarity Trade Union. Since 1994, the palace has been the residence of the President of Poland. Three stone tablets centrally placed behind the chain separating the palace from the street commemorate the tragic Smoleńsk airplane crash of 2010, which killed the then-president Lech Kaczyński, his wife and 94 other passengers including top Polish officials, politicians and military men.

Prince Józef Poniatowski Monument

A large monument in the centre of Presidential Palace's courtyard shows prince Józef Poniatowski, a nephew of Poland's last king Stanisław II Augustus, on a horse with a sword in a hand. The prince was war minister, Duchy of Warsaw military commander and Marshall of the French Empire; he drowned in the Elster river covering the retreat of the French army after the 'Battle of the Nations' at Leipzig (1813). Modelled after the statue of Cesar Marc Aurelius at the Roman Capitol, the monu-

Smoleńsk catastrophe

On April 10th 2010, president Lech Kaczyński, his wife and 94 other Polish top officials took a Tu-154 plane to Smoleńsk in Russia to take part in the 70th anniversary of the Katyń massacre. The poorly equipped Russian military airfield was deep in thick fog. When it approached the runway, the airplane hit the trees and struck the ground, killing all passengers on board. A week of national mourning was declared in Poland as thousands of traumatised Poles wept openly, lit candles and queued for hours to pay their respects to the late president when his body was laid in state at the Presidential Palace. More than 100,000 people took part in the memorial service held on 17 April at the nearby Piłsudski Square. Although the official investigations stated pilot's error as the principal cause of the accident, the tragedy has fuelled many conspiracy theories and became a tool in the subsequent political struggles that have left Polish society deeply divided. The ruling Law and Justice (PiS) party, headed by twin brother of the late president, Jarosław Kaczyński, has announced plans to build yet another monument (besides the one at Powązki cemetery) to the Smoleńsk crash victims and place it near the presidential palace, an idea opposed by city authorities and the city's conservation officer.

Bolesław Prus Monument

ment was officially unveiled in 1923. Destroyed during World War II, it was recast in the 1950s. The remains of the original one can be seen at the Warsaw Uprising Museum (see page 73).

HOTEL BRISTOL

Behind the Presidential Palace rises the legendary **Hotel Bristol ❺**, opened in 1901; one of its original owners was the celebrated pianist and composer – and later, Prime Minister of Poland – Ignacy Paderewski. Famous guests have included Józef Piłsudski ('the father' of Poland's independence), US presidents Richard Nixon and JFK, Margaret Thatcher, Woody Allen and Tina Turner. A classified national monument, it is a superb example of Secessionist architecture and interiors. A coffee in the hotel's Viennese-style café is the least expensive way of enjoying its immense style. On the opposite side of Krakowskie Przedmieście stands the **European Hotel** (Hotel Europejski), another famous hotel built in 1855–78 and for a long time considered the most luxurious in town. Currently under renovation, it is set to reopen later in 2017.

The next building to the right is the modernist **House without Corners** (Dom Bez Kantów) modelled after the neighbouring European Hotel with its curvy façade and built in 1933–5. It is one of the best examples of the so-called Warsaw School of architec-ture. Miraculously, it survived the war, but on some of its walls you can still see holes from bullets.

On the left, hidden among the trees, is the **Bolesław Prus Monument** (Pomnik Bolesława Prusa), a Polish writer, journalist and author of *The Doll*, a masterpiece novel set in Warsaw. Before World War II, a building housing the headquarters of *Kurier Warszawski* (Warsaw's Courier) newspaper – where Prus published his widely-read and praised weekly chronicles – stood on this place.

A little further on is the impressive **Church of the Nuns of the Visitation Order ❻** (Kościół Wizytek), where the young Frederick Chopin would play the organ once a week. The construction of the church took over 100 years (1654–1763), and its interior features a pulpit in the shape of a boat and a beautiful ebony tabernacle. Beyond the church is the nuns' convent, which has barely changed since the 17th century. There is a Chopin bench near the church.

UNIVERSITY OF WARSAW

At Krakowskie Przedmieście Nos 26–28 is the entrance to the **University of Warsaw ❼** (Uniwersytet Warszawski). This aesthetic enclave provides a delightful diversion, animated by the bustle of students arriving for lectures and meeting friends. You enter the campus through a neo-Renaissance gate dating from 1900. Straight ahead is the former Uni-

University of Warsaw's gates

At the Church of the Holy Cross

versity Library, built from 1891 to 1894. Behind the library are the Rector's offices, located in **Kazimierzowski Palace**, a splendid neo-Classical palace, rebuilt in mid-17th century by King Jan Kazimierz (hence the name). In 1765, the College of Chivalry – a secular state-run academy for training military and administrative cadres – was established here, its traditions being continued after 1816 with the establishment of the university.

Across the street from the university gate, at no.7, is the **Bolesław Prus Main Scientific Library** (Główna Księgarnia Naukowa im. B. Prusa). Bolesław Prus set the shop of Stanisław Wokulski – the main protagonist of his novel *The Doll* – in this building. Tucked in the gate you will find a plaque commemorating the other fictional character from Prus' book – Ignacy Rzecki, whose apartment was on the second floor.

At no. 5 is the Rococo **Czapski Palace** ❽ (Pałac Czapskich), used since 1816 as the **Academy of Fine Arts** (Akademia Sztuk Pięknych or ASP). Frederic Chopin lived here with his family until his permanent exile to France in 1830.

Slightly further along Krakowskie Przedmieście rises the baroque façade of the **Church of the Holy Cross** ❾ (Kościół św. Krzyża). After the cathedral, this is the most important church in the history of Warsaw. It was designed from 1679–96, but the façade is more

recent. In the nave, by side pillars, are urns containing the hearts of Frederic Chopin (left) and the writer Władysław Reymont (right), who won the Nobel Prize for literature in 1924. There are also numerous epitaphs of other distinguished writers including Bolesław Prus and Juliusz Słowacki and statesman such as Władysław Sikorski.

STASZIC PALACE

Looking down Krakowskie Przedmieście, your eyes will be drawn to **Staszic Palace** ❿ (Pałac Staszica), a harmonious neo-Classical building designed by Antonio Corazzi in 1820–23. It was the brainchild of the writer and reformer Stanisław Staszic, and was designated as the first headquarters of the Society of Friends of Learning (Towarzystwa Przyjaciół Nauk); it now houses the National Science Academy (Polska Akademia Nauk).

Standing before the palace is a **Monument to Copernicus** ⓫ (Pomnik Mikołaja Kopernika) by the Danish sculptor Bertel Thordvalsen, dating from 1830. In 1944, the Nazis sold the monument for scrap; luckily, it was found before it could be melted down, and after the war was restored to its original position. Look out for the solar system embedded at the foot of the monument.

Left of the monument, across Kopernika street, stands the **Polish Theatre** (Teatr Polski; www.teatrpolski.waw.pl)

Guarding the Tomb of the Unknown Solider

inaugurated in 1913 and restored after the war.

From here you can proceed straight to Route 4 (Nowy Świat and National Museum) or retrace your steps to take Traugutta street between ASP and the Holy Cross Church (there is a Veturilo station at the corner).

ZACHĘTA GALLERY

Follow Traugutta to the small **Mała-chowski Square** (Plac Małachowsk-iego), where – at the corner of Królewska street – you can visit the **Zachęta** ⓬ (pl. Małachowskiego 3; https://zacheta.art.pl; Tue–Sun noon–8pm; free on Thu) – a neo-Renaissance building designed in 1899–1903 that now houses an art gallery hosting exhibitions of modem art. It is one of very few public buildings from the turn of the last century to have survived World War II. In 1922, Poland's first president, Gabriel Narutowicz, was assassinated here.

In the middle of Małachowski Square is the **Protestant Church of the Holy Trinity** (Kościół Ewangelicko-Augsbur-ski św. Trójcy). This circular building, designed in 1777–8 with a 58m- (190ft) high dome and lantern, is frequently used for organ concerts.

At the corner of Kredytowa street and the square is a building dating from 1854–8, designed by the architect Enrico Marconi for the Land Credit Association, but now home to the **Ethnographical Museum** ⓭ (Muzeum Etnograficzne; Kredytowa 1; www.ethnomuseum.pl, Tue, Thu–Fri 10am–5pm, Wed 11am–7pm, Sat 10am–6pm, Sun noon–5pm; free on Thu).

Across Królewska street is the vast **Piłsudski Square** (Plac Piłsudsk-iego). Official state ceremonies are held here, and a changing of the guard takes place in front of the **Tomb of the Unknown Soldier** ⓮ (Grób Niezna-nego Żołnierza); Pope John Paul II also held his first open-air mass in Poland here, in June 1979. The remains of the unknown soldier, who fell in Lwów, were buried here with military honours on 2 November 1925, in a crypt beneath the surviving colonnade of the otherwise non-existent Saxon Palace. Behind the tomb are the **Saxon Gardens** (Ogród Saski), which once abutted the residence of King August II Mocny and his son August III. Laid out in the French style, the gardens formed the backdrop for the city's greatest urban axis of the baroque period. There is another Chopin bench by the tomb.

From the Tomb of Unknown Soldier, continue walking towards the sleek **Metropolitan** building, with its pentagonal glass structure, centred on a circular courtyard with a computer-controlled fountain, which was designed by the British architect, Sir Norman Foster. Hidden behind is a smart restaurant **Michel Moran Bistro de Paris**, see ❷, offering excellent French cuisine.

Turn left into Wierzbowa street, passing a branch of the National Theatre and

Polish National Theatre and Opera House

eventually getting to Teatralny Square (Plac Teatralny)

PLAC TEATRALNY

Dominating the **Teatralny Square** (Plac Teatralny) is the neo-Classical façade of the **Polish National Theatre and Opera House** ⑮ (Teatr Wielki Opera Narodowa; pl. Teatralny 3; http://teatr-wielki.pl; Theatre Museum, entrance from Wierzbowa; by appointment only), which dates from 1825–33. Across the square, the recently reconstructed façade of the former **Town Hall** (Ratusz) hides the offices of several banks.

Turn right into Senatorska, which was Warsaw's main commercial street until the 19th century. Don't miss a plaque embedded on the wall commemorating Krzysztof Kamil Baczyński, a promising young poet who died here at the beginning of the Uprising in 1944.

Follow Senatorska until you see the former **Primate's Palace** (Pałac Prymasowski) on your right; it is now a hotel (ul. Senatorska 13/1; www.hotel bellotto.pl).

If you still have time and feel like visiting the **Museum of Caricature and Cartoon Art** ⑯ (Muzeum Karykatury, Kozia street 11; http://muzeumkary katury.pl; Tue–Sun 10am–6pm; free on Tue) with its rich collection of caricatures dating back to the 18th century, turn right into Kozia street. The green square adjacent to the museum is a peaceful retreat, cut off from the city's hassle and bustle. Exit the museum, retrace your steps to Senatorska street and turn right into Miodowa, which ends at Krakowskie Przedmieście near St Anne Church.

Food and drink

① **PIEROGARNIA**

Bednarska 28/30; tel: 022 828 03 92; daily noon–8pm; www.pierogarnianabednarskiej.pl; €

If you don't mind austere décor with long wooden tables and benches, Pierogarnia – located in the basement of an old tenement – is the place to go in this very touristy part of town. The pierogi has many different fillings: sweet (blueberries, apples, cottage cheese) and salty (cabbage and mushrooms, lentils, minced meat, kasha etc) and the portions are more than generous; in most cases, half a plate will be enough.

② **MICHEL MORAN BISTRO DE PARIS**

Pl. Piłsudskiego 9; tel. 022 826 01 07 www.restaurantbistrodeparis.com; Mon–Fri noon–midnight, Sat 1pm–midnight; €€€

This smart restaurant serves authentic French cuisine by the celebrity chef Michel Moran. It's not cheap, but the fish dishes deserve every penny spent on them. The *foie gras* and desserts are exquisite and the two course set lunch menu (69 PLN/€17) is a good option.

The Copernicus Monument

FROM NOWY ŚWIAT TO ALEJE JEROZOLIMSKIE

Crowded with people and lined with cafés, restaurants, hip bars and glamorous boutiques, Nowy Świat is arguably the most cosmopolitan street in Warsaw and the place to be seen.

DISTANCE: 2.2km (1.3 miles)
TIME: Three hours
START: The Copernicus Monument
END: Palm at the Charles de Gaulle roundabout
POINTS TO NOTE: This is a natural continuation of Route 3 and is easy to combine with Route 5 or Route 9.

The **Copernicus Monument ❶** marks the point at which Krakowskie Przedmieście merges with Nowy Świat street (literally, 'New World'). This has a totally different character, being much narrower and more uniform in style than Krakowskie Przedmieście. Rebuilt after World War II in an early 19th-century neoclassical style, both sides of the street feature attractive façades. As one of the city's smartest shopping destinations, a position it also held in the 1920s and 1930s, the street is home to designer boutiques, jewellers, art galleries and cafés galore. If shops and watering holes are not your cup of tea, you can explore the atmospheric streets that run either parallel or perpendicular to

Nowy Świat, such as Chmielna or Foksal, each of which has its own character and atmosphere.

NOWY ŚWIAT

Start by walking south on the right side of the street until you reach corner of Świętokrzyska street which has recently had a complete makeover. The ground floor of the building at no. 63 is now occupied by the **Warsaw House of Music** (http://nowyswiatmuzyki.pl), a music centre that organises concerts featuring local and international stars and cultural events, as well as daily Chopin recitals at 6pm.

Continue along Nowy Świat, which is lined with numerous restaurants and pavement cafés, where you can stop for a rest. One of the best options for lunch is Specjały Regionalne. Those with a sweet tooth should visit **Blikle**, see ❶, established in 1869 and now occupying an imposing neo-Classical building dating from 1818 (no.33); its interiors are decorated in a *fin-de-siècle* style and it offers the famous *pączki* (doughnuts) filled with rose jam.

Chmielna street

CHMIELNA AND FOKSAL

On the right is pedestrianized **Chmielna** ❷, another popular shopping street. It is being revitalised and several courtyards behind the buildings have been converted into popular restaurants like Mąka i Woda or institutions including Warsaw's branch of the **Goethe Institute** (www. goethe.de/ins/pl/pl/sta/war.html). Before World War II, Chmielna was a street full of cheap hotels, brothels, cabarets and gynecologists' offices. Under communism, it was called Rutkowskiego and was one of the few areas where the communist authorities let private owners

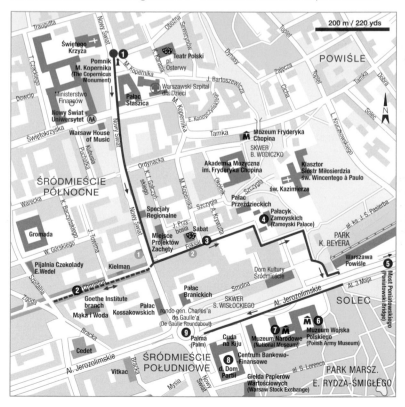

Tank at the Polish Army Museum

run their shops and workshops. A famous shoe shop at no.6 has been in the Kielman family since 1883; even General de Gaulle ordered custom-made shoes here.

Return to Nowy Świat and start exploring **Foksal ③** street, which is almost exactly in front of Chmielna. It is one of very few streets in the city to have preserved something of its pre-war charm. It was once lined with the houses and palaces of the aristocracy; today, these have given way to several fashionable bars and restaurants, including the excellent **Opasły Tom**, see ②, which specialises in modern Polish cuisine. The eastern end of Foksal is crowned by **Zamoyski Palace ④** (Pałacyk Zamoyskich), a French Renaissance-style building designed by Leandro Marconi in 1878–9 and one of few late 19th-century Warsaw residences to have survived the war. It now houses a restaurant. Going through the passage to the right of the palace, and then turning right along the edge of the bluff (which offers a nice view of the city), you reach the busy Jerozolimskie Avenue. To cross this busy thoroughfare with a tramline in the centre, go down the stairs leading to the platforms of Warszawa Powiśle railway station, and then turn right to pass under Poniatowski bridge (unfortunately, one of the dirtiest spots in the city). **Poniatowski Bridge ⑤** (Most Poniatowskiego) was opened in 1914. It was designed by Mieczysław Marszewski and Wacław Paszkowski, with Stefan Szyller contributing the Polish Renaissance-style architectural framework.

THE NATIONAL MUSEUM

The modernist building in front of the exit was built in 1927–1938 with the museum in mind and its monumental form makes it a popular film setting for works about Nazi Germany. Its eastern wing houses the **Polish Army Museum ⑥** (Muzeum Wojska Polskiego; Jerozolimskie 3; www.muzeumwp.pl; Wed 10am–5pm, Thu–Sun 10am–4pm, outdoor display in summer daily 9am–6pm, winter until 4pm; free on Sat), which has an outdoor display of tanks, guns and aeroplanes. Inside, the permanent exhibition traces the thousand-year history of Polish warfare. Highlights include 17th-century Hussar (winged cavalry) armour and an Ottoman tent captured at Vienna in 1683.

Next is the **National Museum ⑦** (Muzeum Narodowe; Jerozolimskie 3, www.mnw.art.pl; Tue–Wed, Fri–Sun 10am–6pm, Thu 10am–8pm; free on Tue), small but definitely worth seeing. The highlights include a unique set of frescoes from the Nubian town of Farras, obtained during archaeological excavations in the Sudan; the largest gallery of medieval art in Poland; and a recently renovated gallery of Old Masters presenting paintings, sculptures and decorative arts together. A superb collection of Polish paintings from the beginning of the modem era until the interwar period contains the work of artists such as Jan Matejko, painter of the enormous *Battle of Grunwald (Tannenberg)*, Jacek

National Museum exhibit   *The Palm*

Malczewski, Józef Chełmoński and Stanisław Wyspiański.

Leaving the National Museum, go towards the imposing **Dom Partii** ❽ – the former headquarters of the Polish United Workers' Party (the Communist Party), raised from 1948 to 1951. After 1989, this seat of communist power was transformed into a symbol of capitalism – the **Warsaw Stock Exchange**, later relocated to a contemporary building on nearby Książęca street. Under the arcades of Dom Partii are two cubicles made of glass, which house a restaurant and pub, Cuda na Kiju, offering an excellent choice of Polish craft beers.

DE GAULLE ROUNDABOUT

Leaving Dom Partii, turn left to reach **De Gaulle Roundabout** (Rondo de Gaulle'a) at the corner of Jerozolimskie Avenue and Nowy Świat. The monument of the marching French president, unveiled in 2005, is a copy of his monument standing on the Champs Élysées in Paris. Some joke that De Gaulle is rushing to one of the numerous cafés nearby. In the middle of the roundabout stands an artificial 12-meter (39ft-) high **Palm** ❾. Joanna Rajkowska's artistic provocation (the palm was a link with Jerusalem, which gave the name to the avenue Jerozolimskie, and a symbol of the vacuum created by the disappearance of Jews and their culture from Warsaw) has stirred controversy. However, the palm has become one of the city's landmarks.

Food and drink

❶ BLIKLE

Nowy Świat 35; tel: 669 609 706; www.blikle.pl; daily 9am–8pm; €€

Founded in 1869, this is a true institution among Warsaw pastry shops. It has witnessed the ups and downs of the city and tried to make the latter more palatable to Varsovians. This pastry shop and adjacent café was always located at Nowy Świat 35, though there are dozens of branches in Warsaw and other Polish towns. For many Varsovians, Blikle's pączki (doughnuts) are set the standard. It would be a shame, however, not to try other delicacies from the long and varied menu. The company prides itself on not adding any preservatives, emulators, sweeteners or flavour enhancers to its products.

❷ OPASŁY TOM

Foksal 17; tel. 022 621 18 81; http://kregliccy.pl/opaslytom; daily noon–10pm; €€€

Situated in a former bookstore of the famous Polish publisher, PWN, this is a small place with real cuisine d'auteur by chef Klaudia Borawska. The menu is short and seasonal and all the ingredients are fresh and local. Lamb stuffed pierogi are delicious and it's also a good place to sample some Polish wines and cheeses. Though expensive, the five course degustation menu is good value at 125zł.

The Church of St Alexander on Three Crosses Square

FROM TRZECH KRZYŻY SQUARE TO NA ROZDROŻU SQUARE

Take a leisurely stroll along the stylish Aleje Ujazdowskie, a picture-postcard boulevard in the heart of town, lined with foreign embassies, fin-de-siècle villas and wonderful parks.

DISTANCE: 3.3km (2 miles)
TIME: Three hours
START: Trzech Krzyży Square
END: Na Rozdrożu Square
POINTS TO NOTE: This is a continuation of Route 4. It can be easily followed by Route 6.

The following section of the Royal Route takes you through the elegant Three Crosses Square, with its exclusive retail stores, modern hotels and string of trendy cafés and restaurants, to Ujazdowskie Avenue (Aleje Ujazdowskie), considerably wider and busier than Nowy Świat.

THREE CROSSES SQUARE

Just beyond the De Gaulle roundabout, Nowy Świat leads you onto the **Three Crosses Square ❶** (Plac Trzech Krzyży), one of the most fashionable places in Warsaw. In the communist era, this was a cruising area for the city's gay community; today the square is home to a plethora of cafés, shops, and luxurious housing developments. The round-domed building in the middle of the square is the **Church of St Alexander** (Kościół św. Aleksandra), designed in 1818–25. Just beside the church are two granite columns topped by gilded crosses, which flank a late-baroque **Monument of St John Nepomuk**, who is shown holding another cross; these three crosses give the square its name (ignoring the fact that there are two other crosses on the church's façade).

A string of cafés line the northern side of the square, whereas the eastern corner is occupied by a modern brick building with exclusive retail shops under its colonnade. Nearby, across Książęca, is the sleek seat of the **Warsaw Stock Exchange**. At Nos 4–6 on the square stands the classicist building of the **Deaf-Mute Institute**, opened in 1827.

The square marks the start of the **Ujazdowskie Avenue**, one of Warsaw's most elegant streets, lined with fin-de-siècle villas and luxury mansion blocks. The avenue's origins go back to 1724–31 when King Augustus II the Strong ordered the construction of the Cavalry Road. In the 18th and 19th centuries

The Giants House

the area became fashionable with aristocrats, entrepreneurs and industrial moguls, who built palaces and mansions along the street; these were later occupied by foreign embassies or the headquarters for foreign legations, and have been renovated following devastation during World War II.

Of particular note is the **Giants' House** ❷ (Dom Pod Gigantami) at no. 24, just at the beginning of the avenue, built in 1908, with a neoclassical façade and a small balcony supported by two powerful atlantes. Today it houses Restaurant Pod Gigantami. Nearby is another pit-stop opportunity – the excellent Georgian restaurant **Rusico**, see ❶.

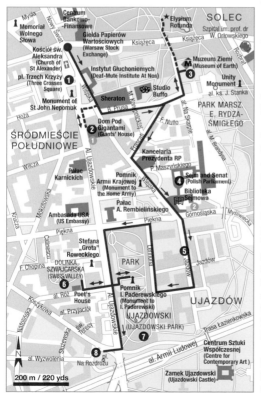

MUSEUM OF EARTH

However, before you delve into Ujazdowskie Avenue, it's worth making a little detour to the **Museum of Earth** ❸ (Muzeum Ziemi; Na Skarpie 20/26/27, www.mz.pan.pl; Mon–Fri 9am–4pm; Sun 10am–4pm; free on Sun). To reach the museum, turn left into Bolesława Prusa street, leaving the monument of the peasant leader Wicenty Witos on your right. Walk along past the Sheraton Hotel and just before the park, turn left into an alley, which leads to the museum, located in the former residence of Prince Poniatowski.

It consists of two parts: to the left, a palace; to the right, a summer palace of 1781, with a large

Monument to the Home Army

columned salon which is open on one side. A gently descending Doric colonnade has been preserved from the **Summer Palace**, which the architect Bohdan Pniewski integrated into his own modernist villa in 1935–39. Today, the building is one of the most interesting examples of 1930s architecture; a notable curiosity is the marble stairway stained with the blood of an insurgent injured during the Warsaw Uprising. The collection of Baltic amber is of particular interest and is one of the largest in the world.

The suspended footbridge that crosses Książęca street beyond the museum leads to the other part of **Śmigły Rydz Park**, which stretches until the complex of the National and Polish Army Museums (see Route 4). Walking among trees along the edge of the bluff, it is hard to imagine that before 1939 this was an industrial district full of factory buildings. The former entrance to the underground **Elysium Rotunda** (rotunda Elizeum; closed for public) is visible on the slopes of the bluff, a feature of the landscaped park created here in the 1770s for the king's brother, Prince Kazimierz Poniatowski, who had a reputation as a wastrel and a womaniser.

SEJM

Go back and proceed along Frascati to the junction with Wiejska street and turn left. Beyond the huge **Monument to the Home Army** (Pomnik Armii Krajowej), established in 1999, are the buildings of the lower and upper houses of the **Polish Parliament** ❹ (Sejm and Senat); the rotunda of the assembly chamber was designed in 1925–28 by Kazimierz Skórewicz.

JAZDÓW

At the end of Wiejska you could turn left to refuel at **Brasserie Warszawska**, see ❷, or cross Piękna and continue straight into Jazdów street to explore **Jazdów** ❺ – a settlement of 27 wooden Finnish houses, created at the back of Ujazdowski Garden in 1945. The houses were part of the war reparations that Finland was forced to pay on behalf of the Soviet Union. Initially, they offered a temporary housing for the employees of the Capital's Reconstruction Bureau. Only a few dozen have survived and in 2011, a heated debated began over plans of the city authorities to demolish the remaining houses. The inhabitants' resistance – supported by the Finnish Ambassador – saved the historic settlement and gave birth to the association of its residents and friends: **Open Jazdów** (Otwarty Jazdów, http://jazdow.pl/en), which organises a series of cultural events each year. It is particularly pleasant to walk around this peaceful, almost country-like neighbourhood in the summer.

PIĘKNA AND THE SWISS VALLEY

Return to Piękna street and head left past the French, Canadian and German

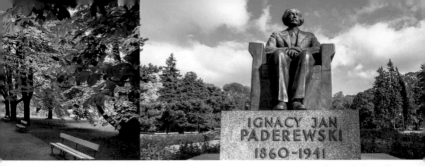

Ujazdowski Park　　　　　　　　　　　　　*Ignacy Paderewski statue*

embassies to reach Ujazdowskie Avenue. Across the street is the modern **US embassy** (No's 29–31), looking rather out of place among the elegant villas. Before 1989, the embassy was often besieged by crowds of people queueing from the early hours to apply for American visas. Cross Piękna Street and continue south. A huge boulder on your left commemorates a successful execution of Warsaw's SS and police chief Franz Kutshera on February 1944 by the elite unit of the Home Army (AK). In revenge, the Nazis killed 300 Poles.

Further on the right, is the **Swiss Valley** ❻ (Dolina Szwajcarska), an elegant garden created in 1786, later turned into an entertainment park. At the end of 19th century it had the most stylish ice ring in Warsaw. Unfortunately, only a small section of the garden has survived to the present day. After World War II, the prestigious **Aleja Róż** street was home to many communist apparatchiks as well as the literati. At no.6 is the so called 'Poet's House', where famous poets including Konstanty Ildefons Gałczyński, Władysław Broniewski and Antoni Słonimski lived.

UJAZDOWSKI PARK

On the other side of Ujazdowskie Avenue is the **Ujazdowski Park** ❼. Just beyond the entrance gate, you can weigh yourself on a set of antique scales, which have stood here since 1912 and are noted for their accuracy. It has been a public park since the end of 19th century, at that time one of the most modern in Europe. It is a peaceful retreat, offering a much welcome respite from the city buzz. A monument to the famous 20th century Polish pianist, composer and statesman Ignacy Paderewski is centrally located. Park Ujazdowski borders with **Na Rozdrożu Square** ❽.

Food and drink

❶ RUSIKO

Al. Ujazdowskie 22; tel: 022 629 06 28; Tue–Sun noon–11pm; http://rusiko.pl; €€-€€€
This family restaurant has a friendly ambience and modern ethnic décor, and serves the most popular Georgian staples: khakapuli (lamb stew), khachapuri (cheese-filled bread) and khinkali (dumplings). The excellent Georgian wines are not to be missed.

❷ BRASSERIE WARSZAWSKA

Górnośląska 24; tel: 022 628 94 23; Mon–Sat noon–10pm, Sun until 8pm; www.brasseriewarszawska.pl; €€€€
Inspired by Varsovian tradition and the European present, this stylish restaurant's menu skillfully blends simplicity and elegance; however, calling it a simple brasserie is a huge understatement. With its crisp linen tablecloths, shiny cutlery and artistic presentation of food, it is definitely a top-notch culinary establishment. Extensive wine list.

The Palace on the Island

ŁAZIENKI PARK

Dotted with palaces, pavilions, orangeries, cafés and restaurants, Łazienki Park is a magical place where you can easily spend an entire day strolling the peaceful paths, watching peacocks, swans and ducks in the pond, or listening to a Chopin concert.

DISTANCE: 5.4km (3.3 miles)
TIME: Four hours
START: Na Rozdrożu Square
END: Belweder Palace
POINTS TO NOTE: Chopin concerts are held on Sundays. The park closes at 9pm. Entrance to the museums in the park is free of charge on Thursdays.

Łazienki Park is a favourite place for the people of Warsaw to relax and unwind, and while visitor numbers obviously peak in the summer months, the park is popular all year round for its sheer beauty. The park is also a perfect setting for summer Chopin concerts.

UJAZDOWSKI CASTLE AND BOTANICAL GARDEN

The **Na Rozdrożu Square** (Plac Na Rozdrożu) is located, as its name ('at the crossroads') suggests, at a confluence of several important communication thoroughfares, including Ujazdowskie, Jan Chrystian Szuch and Wyzwolenia

Avenues. To get to **Ujazdowski Castle ❶** (Zamek Ujazdowski), pass the Rozdroże Cafe, located inside a rather ugly Social-realist glass pavilion, turn left and go past the excellent **Atelier Amaro** restaurant – the first one in Poland to be awarded a Michelin star. This former royal residence was built at the beginning of the 17th century for King Zygmunt III Vasa and his son Władysław IV, burnt down during World War II and foolishly dismantled in 1953, only to be reconstructed 20 years later. Today, the castle accommodates a **Centre for Contemporary Art** (Centrum Sztuki Współczesnej; Ujazdowskie 6, http://u-jazdowski.pl; Tue–Wed, Fri–Sun noon–7pm; Thu noon–9pm), which holds concerts and interesting art exhibitions. You can eat here at the popular **Qchnia Artystyczna** restaurant, see ❶, which has fantastic views over Agrykola Park and the Vistula river from its backyard terrace.

Return to Aleje Ujazdowskie along Agrykola street, on which one of Warsaw's last surviving gaslights can be seen. Aleje Ujazdowskie continues on to the University of Warsaw's small, but interesting

Strolling in the park   *Monument to Chopin*

Botanical Garden ❷ (Ogród Botaniczny, www.garden.uw.edu.pl; only Apr–Oct), established in 1824. The opposite side of the avenue is lined with monotonous government buildings (including the chancellery of the Prime Minister).

ŁAZIENKI PARK

Beyond the garden is the main entrance gate to **Łazienki Park ❸** (Łazienki Królewskie; www.lazienki-krolewskie.pl; daily until 9pm, buildings summer daily 10am–6pm, winter Mon 11am–4pm, Tue–Sun 10am–4pm), one of the most beautiful parks in Europe with several idyllic spots, as well as charming buildings that hark back to the reign of Poland's last king – Stanisław August Poniatowski (see box). Łazienki has been open to the public since 1863.

Hunting grounds existed here as early as the Middle Ages, and in the 17th century, at the foot of the bluff, was a royal game reserve filled with aurochs (an extinct species of long-horned wild ox). In 1674, Stanislaw Herakliusz Lubomirski, the Grand Marshal of the Crown, built a garden retreat here with an eccentric bathhouse (*łazienka*) on an island. But it was Stanislaw August Poniatowski, Poland's last king, who commissioned Johann Christian Schuch, a landscape gardener from Dresde, to lay out the vast royal gardens that have survived to this day.

Regulations

Before entering the park, it is worth taking notice of rather stiff regulations that include the prohibi-

tion of sitting on the immaculate lawns and riding a bicycle, among others. For-

The philosopher king

The last king of Poland, Stanisław August Poniatowski (1732–1798) is a highly controversial figure. As a ruler who oversaw the country's partition by its powerful neighbours, he is often portrayed by his critics as a weak art lover and womaniser. Indeed, throughout his long life he had women galore. Among his lovers was the Russian Empress Katherine the Great (before she gained her title) whose support turned out crucial for him to be elected King of Poland in 1764. As a monarch, he pushed for reform, trying to transform the country into a modern constitutional monarchy, a process which culminated in the passing of the 3rd of May Constitution in 1791, the first in Europe. In an attempt to strengthen the army, he founded the College of Chivalry (Szkołę Rycerską), an elite school for royal cadets. He also believed that by promoting culture, arts education and Enlightenment ideals he would be able to shape the 'nation's spiritual culture'. His plans were opposed by some of the Polish and Lithuanian nobles, not to mention Prussia, Russia and Austria, who were eager to keep their neighbour as weak as possible. Following three partitions of Poland (1772, 1793 and 1795), Stanisław August was left with no kingdom and had to abdicate. He died in exile in 1798.

tunately, it is possible to run in the park early in the morning and there are two picnic areas near Belvedere restaurant and at the Southern end of the park. It is also forbidden to feed animals (though this is not strictly enforced). The fauna of the park comprises swans, peacocks, hedgehogs, ducks, roe deers and red squirrels as well as wild water birds including mallards, mandarin ducks, swans, goosanders, common moorhens, Eurasian coots, black-headed gulls, Eurasian widgeons, gadwalls and greater white-fronted geese.

Chopin monument

Past the main entrance gate, the **Monument to Chopin** stands in the middle of a rose garden – one of the most beautiful Secessionist monuments in Europe, designed in 1908, but not unveiled until 1926 due to opposition by the Tsarist authorities. The current monument is a reconstruction, as the original was destroyed by Nazis in 1940. Concerts of Chopin's music take place here on Sundays in the summer (noon and 4pm).

Old Orangerie and Royal Theatre

Go left from the gate, past the modern **Monument to Henryk Sienkiewicz**, and descend from the bluff along a broad alley. You will come to a long building with large arcaded windows and a garden full of orange trees, which is the beautifully restored **Old Orangery** (Stara Pomarańczarnia), designed and built by the royal architect Dominik

The Palace on the Island is a must-see

Merlini in 1774–7. The **Royal Theatre** (Teatr Królewski) is housed in the building's east wing. It is one of Europe's few remaining 18th-century court theatres, featuring a wooden interior decorated with murals. Equally interesting is the **Royal Sculpture Gallery** designed by Johann Chrystian Kammsetzer, embodying King Stanisław August's idea of a modern public museum. Copies of the most famous ancient sculptures (*The Laocoon Group* and *Apollo Belvedere*, among others) are displayed against a background of trompe l'oeil architecture and an idyllic Italian landscape to resemble alleys of statues in Italian gardens.

Palace on the Island

Continuing along the main alley, you reach the **White Pavilion** (Bialy Dom), a small villa built in 1774–7 as a residence for the king's sisters. It houses the surviving part of Stanisław August's Collection of Prints (closed for renovation).

Visible further on is the **Palace on the Island** (Pałac na Wyspie) also known as the Palace on the Water (Pałac na Wodzie). Situated on an artificial island, this is one of the greatest monuments in Poland, modest in its proportions but of great artistic sophistication. Initially a 17th-century bathhouse belonging to Grand Marshal Lubomirski, it was later remodelled to serve as the summer residence of King Stanisław August Poniatowski.

Fine 17th-century bas-reliefs have survived in Lubomirski's bathroom, where large sections of the walls are covered in Delft tiles. Impressive, too, are the ballroom, with marble chimney pieces in the form of porticoes, the **Picture Gallery**, containing part of Poniatowski's art collection, the **King's bedroom** and the huge **Solomon Hall**, the principal reception room. It was in the **dining room**, in the years 1771–82, that the king would hold his famous 'Thursday dinners' in the company of artists, writers and scholars.

Leaving the palace terrace, which is decorated with stone allegorical figures of the Bug and Vistula rivers, you come to the **Grand Annexe** (Wielka Oficyna). During the period of the Congress Kingdom, the building housed a famous **Officer Cadet School**. On the night of 29 November 1830, a group of college cadets marched on Belvedere Palace to begin the November Uprising.

Myślewicki Palace

At the end of the pond, beyond **The Old Guardhouse** is the **Jan III Sobieski Monument**. Commissioned in 1788 by Poniatowski, it shows Sobieski as the vanquisher of the Ottoman Turks, proudly astride his mare and trampling enemies underfoot.

Behind the Grand Annexe is the semicircular façade of the compact **Myślewicki Palace**, designed by Domenico Merlini. It played an important role in 1958–70 as the venue of a series of meetings between diplomats from communist China and the US, which helped to establish a dialogue and mutual trust between the two countries.

Theatre on the Isle

Those interested in the subject might wish to make a brief detour to the **Museum of Hunting and Equestrianism** (Muzeum Łowiectwa i Jeździectwa), a short distance from the palace. You can then go back to the pond to see the excellent **Theatre on the Isle** (Teatr Na Wyspie), designed by royal architect, Johann Chrystian Kammsetzer and whose late 18th-century stage is an imitation of the ancient temple; the crest of the amphitheatre is decorated with eight statues of poets, made by Stanisław Jakubowski in the 1920s.

Passing the picturesque bridge southeast from the theatre, you reach the **New Orangery** (Nowa Pomarańczarnia), a cast-iron-and-glass structure designed in 1860 at a time when Łazienki belonged to the Tsars of Russia. Inside, lush greenery and exotic plants provide an atmospheric setting for the **Belvedere restaurant**, see ❷, one of Warsaw's finest.

The expansive lawns and ancient trees near the New Orangery merge almost imperceptibly with a romantic garden adjacent to the **Belvedere Palace**. Walk up and on your left you will see the picturesque view of the Egyptian Temple. Go around the edge of the pond and climb back up to the top of the bluff, passing the **Temple of the Sybil** (closed), in the form of a miniature Greek temple.

Belvedere Palace ❹ (individual tours on the last Sat of the month, via 'Europa-Travel'; belweder@europa-travel.pl; free), was thoroughly remodelled in 1819–22 to serve as the residence of the hated Tsarist governor of Warsaw, the Grand Duke Constantine, brother of Tsar Alexander I. After Poland regained her independence, the Belvedere became the official residence of Polish heads of state. The tours include an exhibition devoted to Marshal Józef Piłsudski, the room depicting the history of the War Order of Virtuti Militari, the Belvedere Chapel and selected historical rooms.

Food and drink

❶ KUCHNIA ARTYSTYCZNA

Jazdów 2; daily noon–10pm; tel: 022 625 7627; http://qchnia.pl; €€€
The beautiful location and a terrace on a high bluff overseeing the park is a key asset of this café cum restaurant. The seasonal menu changes frequently and is very creative, just like the chef – Magda Gessler – who is one of the brightest stars in Warsaw's gastronomic sky. In summer, try to get a table on the terrace: there is no better place to eat al fresco in town.

❷ BELVEDERE

ul. Agrykoli 1; tel. 022 558 67 01; www.belvedere.com.pl; Mon–Fri noon–4pm, 6–11pm, Sat noon–11pm, Sun noon–8pm; €€€€
Located in Lazienki Park's New Orangery, the short but impressive menu here includes herring, beef tartare, boar stew and duck. In summer you can enjoy the open air setting in the beautiful surroundings of the park.

View over Mariensztat from St Anne's Church

POWIŚLE

Powiśle, an area close to the riverbank, is currently one of the most sought–after addresses in Warsaw. The University of Warsaw Library and its popular roof garden, the Copernicus Science Centre and the regenerated riverbank have all turned this into a thriving neighbourhood.

DISTANCE: 3.7km (2.3 miles)
TIME: A packed half day or a leisurely day (especially if you visit museums or make longer stops at the parks or riverbank)
START: Sigismund's Column
END: Museum of Chopin
POINTS TO NOTE: This route should be avoided on Mondays when museums are closed. It could be easily preceded by Route 1 or followed by Route 4. Note that in winter, the BUW garden closes at 3pm.

Once a neighbourhood of fishermen, small artisans, Jewish merchants and workers, left somewhat neglected following the fall of communism, Powiśle has undergone a remarkable transformation over the last decade. The district now abounds with elegant housing developments, which offer breathtaking views over the river, state-of-the art museums and Warsaw University's main library with a fabulous roof garden. Numerous cafés, bars and restaurants are always full of people, mostly students, chatting their breaks away over lattes and espressos or working on their laptops. The renovated riverbank, where several bars open in summer and a picturesque cycling path runs along the Vistula river, adds to Powiśle's charm.

MARIENSZTAT

Overlooking the Castle Square (see page 30), **Sigismund's Column ❶**, is a favourite meeting point for locals. Go to the stone balustrade to the right of the Royal Castle for a quick look across the Vistula river. Weather permitting, on the other side you will see the Praga district, with the imposing basket-like silhouette of the PGE National Stadium (see page 105). Below lies the usually jammed Trasa W-Z (East-West Route). Go down the steps hidden behind the bell tower and turn right into a narrow alley leading down to **Mariensztat's Market Square ❷** (Rynek Mariensztacki).

Before World War II, this was Powiśle's principal marketplace, dating back to the second half of the 18th century (it took its name from the owner, a Polish aristo-

Warsaw University's library roof garden

crat called Maria Potocka – *Marienstadt* in German means Mary's Town). Unfortunately, none of the original buildings survive – nearly the whole district was razed to the ground during the Warsaw Uprising. After the war, a new housing estate, the first in the post-war capital, was completed in 1949 in the same place. From here, turn right and follow Sowia street.

Bednarska Street

After less than 200 metres (656ft) you will reach Bednarska, a steep cobblestone street leading up to Krakowskie

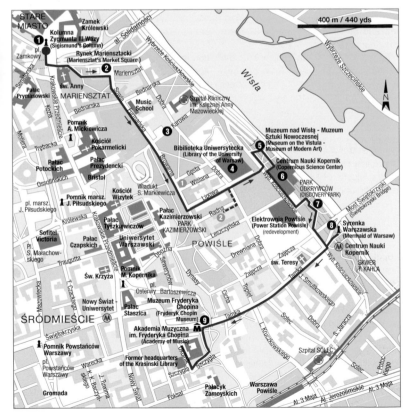

Bridge at the roof garden

Przedmieście (see page 44). If you feel like it, you can climb it to see a few historic townhouses (in the upper section) which miraculously survived the war. Otherwise continue on Furmańska until you reach the corner with **Karowa ❸**. On your right, a massive grey modern building with three flags in front of it is the seat of the National Security Bureau. Winding and steep Karowa street is where the final stage of the popular winter car rally (Rajd Barbórki) takes place at the beginning of December. The event draws crowds of car-mad Varsovians and offers an opportunity to see the best Polish and international drivers in action.

Continue across the street along Browarna. You might consider boosting your energy at **Boscaiola**, see ❶. After refuelling, follow Lipowa past the sleek building of the Faculty of Modern Languages to reach the university library.

LIBRARY OF THE UNIVERSITY OF WARSAW

Popularly known as BUW (an abbreviation of its Polish name), the **Library of the University of Warsaw ❹** (Bibilioteka Uniwersytecka, Dobra 56/66; www.buw. uw.edu.pl; Mon–Fri 8am–10pm, Sat 9am–9pm, Sun 3–8pm) is an architectural gem designed by Marek Budzyński and Zbigniew Badowski and opened in 1999. It consists of two buildings connected by a glass-roofed passage. A huge open book with an inscription 'Hinc Omnia' ('hence all') is poised above the entrance to the four-store main building, which boasts an impressive collection of 3 million titles. A huge, curved green façade on Dobra street houses large blocks with different classical texts by Plato, Polish Renaissance poet Jan Kochanowski and excerpts from the Book of Ezequiel in Hebrew. The main lecture hall, open to the public, is protected by an amazing glass dome.

However, the BUW's biggest attraction is by far the beautiful **garden** (daily Apr and Oct 8am–6pm, May–Sept 8am–8pm, Nov–Mar 8am–3pm with no access to the roof; free), the largest in Europe. It spreads over an area of more than 1 hectare (2.5 acres) and is divided into an upper and lower part, connected by a stream and a water cascade. The lower part includes a small fish pond and is often used as an open-air art gallery with works of various Polish and international artists spread across the immaculate lawns. The upper part, covering the roof of the library building, boasts a network of beautifully arranged paths, bridges and pergolas overgrown with frost-resistant vine. It also offers amazing views. Visitors can even peer inside the library through strategically placed windows or the glass roof. The garden is a perfect place for a short rest where you can sit on a bench and relax.

If you feel hungry, continue south on Dobra Street and then turn right into small and picturesque Radna Street. **Dziurka od Klucza**, see ❷, specialises in home-made pasta.

MUSEUM OF MODERN ART

Go back to Lipowa street and head towards the river. Walk along the library's wall. Across the street on the river bank is a white rectangular pavilion housing the temporary site of the **Museum of Modern Art** ❺ (Muzeum Sztuki Nowoczesnej http://artmuseum.pl; Tue–Thu noon–8pm, Fri noon–10pm, Sat 11am–8pm, Sun 11am–6pm; free). Inside the pavilion (which already housed Berlin's Kunsthalle in years 2008–2010), designed by Austrian architect Adolf Krischanitz, there is an exhibition hall, a bookstore and a small education centre. At the opposite site of the entrance, a nice café with an outdoor wooden terrace (open in summer) offers superb views over the river. The long façade on the riverside is entirely covered with a work by Polish artist Sławomir Pawszak. If you need a break, there is a special Innogy bench near museum where you can charge your smartphone with solar energy and use WiFi. Regenerated, take a short walk along the river to the nearby shrine to science.

COPERNICUS SCIENCE CENTER

Hands down the most popular of Warsaw's museums at present, **Copernicus Science Centre** ❻ (Centrum Nauki Kopernik; Apr–Jun Tue–Fri 8am–6pm and Sat–Sun 10am–7pm; Jul–Aug Tue–Sun 9am–7pm; Sept–Dec Tue–Fri 9am–6pm and Sat–Sun 10am–7pm; www.kopernik.org.pl) received a record number of 1.1 million visitors in 2016. The ever expanding permanent exhibitions include amazing hands-on displays, multimedia presentations, logical puzzles and simulators (the earthquake platform is very realistic!) that can keep children as well as grown-ups busy all day.

Prepare to be amazed by the fire tornado, learn about human emotions and experience different kinds of electromagnetic radiation in nine permanent galleries. The official premise, 'we don't look, we experiment' defines the philosophy behind brilliant exhibits either built by the centre's specialists or commissioned with the world's best engineers. Enthusiastic staff members conduct mini-workshops, carry out experiments and engage with visitors, offering exhaustive explanations. There are also labs, lectures, concerts and a top-notch planetarium (www.niebokopernika.pl) with 3D films and laser shows for adults and children. Relaxation areas, a café and large restaurant on the ground floor provide a much needed respite and prevent sensory overload, while a **roof garden** (Tue–Sun May–Aug 10am–8pm, Sept–Oct 10am–5pm) offers splendid views over the river and towards the National Stadium.

DISCOVERY PARK

Exit the museum and head left through the adjacent **Discovery Park** ❼, a green area by the river where science picnics, concerts, open-air cinema shows, sky observations and many other events are

The Copernicus Science Center and the Museum of Modern Art on the banks of the Vistula

held in summer. You can also experiment with sounds, using the outdoor exhibits.

Opposite the park is the fenced off area containing the closed **Powiśle power station**, constructed in 1904. It provided electric power to the Polish held districts during the Warsaw Uprising and was a location of fierce fighting. Destroyed by the Germans, it was rebuilt after the war and served the city until the beginning of the 1990s. Currently, the area around the power station is being converted into a modern complex. Leave the Discovery Park and cross busy Zajęcza street, heading straight to the metro entrance. On the left, you will see the impressive tower of the cable-stayed **Świętokrzyski Bridge** (Most Świętokrzyski). Opened in 2000, its deck is supported by 48 cables and two piers (on the left bank of the river). Turn left before the metro entrance and continue towards the river until you see the Mermaid of Warsaw (*Syrenka Warszawska*) monument.

SYRENKA

Armed with a sword in one hand and a shield in the other, the **Mermaid ❽** has been the symbol of Warsaw since the end of the 14th century, when it first appeared on a royal seal as a man with wings, the legs of an ox and a lion's tail. In its current form of half-woman, half-fish, it is present on the city's coat of arms, buses and trams, and countless souvenirs. Designed by artist Ludwika Nitschowa, the monument was unveiled in 1939. It escaped the German siege of the city and the Warsaw Uprising in 1944 almost unscathed. Always a popular place for walks and taking pictures, *Syrenka* was thoroughly cleaned and renovated in 2016. A fountain around the pedestal was also added.

Frederick Chopin

Frederick (Fryderyk) Chopin was introduced to piano by his mother. At six he started taking regular lessons and two years later he gave his first public piano concert in Warsaw, his home. After hearing Chopin play at concerts in Vienna, German composer Robert Schumann famously said: 'Hats off, gentlemen! A genius'. Soon after he turned twenty, Chopin left Warsaw and never returned. He eventually settled down in Paris where his social circle included many prominent musicians, including Franz Liszt, and the love of his life, the French writer George Sand. Their intense relationship resulted in her nursing Chopin for several years after he contracted tuberculosis (it is now argued he also suffered from cystic fibrosis). She finally left him in 1847 when he was seriously ill and virtually penniless. A highly successful visit to London briefly revived his fortunes, where he gave his final public concert in 1848. Chopin died a year later in his Paris home in the Place Vendome. As he wished, his heart was brought to Poland and inserted into a pillar of Warsaw's Holy Cross Church.

Exhibition hall at the Fryderyk Chopin Museum

The monument is close to the regenerated riverbank, where there are paths for walkers and bikers. In summer, you can follow it south to find several riverside clubs and bars popular with hipsters.

FRYDERYK CHOPIN MUSEUM

Leave the river behind and head back past the metro station. Cross Wybrzeże Kościuszkowskie street and walk up Tamka street towards the city centre for about 800 metres (2,625ft) to get to **Ostrogski Palace**, now the seat of the **Fryderyk Chopin Museum ❾** (Muzeum Fryderyka Chopina; Tue–Sun 11am–8pm; free on Sun; http://chopin.museum/ en). Reopened after a long restoration for the 200th anniversary of Frederick Chopin's birth, the rich collection of more than 7,500 exhibits is spread across four floors of the palace and includes valuable manuscripts, prints, personal letters, photographs and even his calligraphy exercise book. The interactive multimedia displays cover the history and works of the great composer. The museum also organises tours to its branch in **Żelazowa Wola** (tel: 046-863 33 00; Tue–Sun Apr–Sept 9am–7pm, Oct–Mar 9am–5pm; Mon park only), where Chopin was born in 1810.

Walking parallel to the bluff, you will reach, at Okólnik street, a low 1960s building with the sound of trumpets and trombones emanating from its windows. This is the **Academy of Music** (Akademia Muzyczna im. Fryderyka Chopina). There is an abandoned building with a monumental colonnade: the former headquarters of the **Krasinski Library**. After the defeat of the Warsaw Uprising, the Nazis burnt the priceless collections brought here from libraries all over Warsaw.

The striking facade of the Museum of the History of Polish Jews

JEWISH WARSAW

This walk, just north of the city centre, covers the site of the infamous Jewish Ghetto and explores the remains of the once flourishing culture that was sentenced to extinction by the Nazi occupiers.

DISTANCE: 8.1km (5 miles)
TIME: A full day
START: PAST-a Building
END: Umschlagplatz
POINTS TO NOTE: The POLIN museum is closed on Tue; Pawiak opens only Wed–Sun; Hala Mirowska is best visited on a weekday.

Before World War II the Jewish community accounted for around one-third of Warsaw's population – and was the largest in Europe. It was a diversified community composed of three main groups: Hasidic Jews, Orthodox Jews and a small but influential minority of Polonised Jewish intelligentsia and bourgeoisie. In November 1940, the Nazis began rounding up and confining Jews to the ghetto, a district of about 4 sq km (1.5 sq miles). Ultimately, over 400,000 Jews were enclosed, where they endured inhumane conditions, suffering inevitably from overcrowding, disease and starvation. Even the Nazis realised that the situation was untena-ble and started transporting Jews from the Warsaw ghetto to the death camps of Auschwitz and Treblinka, until only about 60,000 remained.

In April 1943, the resistance movement led by the Jewish Combat Organisation (ŻOB) culminated in a month-long uprising. The Jewish fighters desperately fought the overwhelming German forces for nearly a month, but being poorly armed, could not withstand the onslaught of regular German troops that used flame throwers and explosives to destroy entire blocks of buildings. Some 7,000 fighters were killed; only a handful survived by escaping through a network of sewer canals to the 'Aryan' part of the city, where they were picked up by the Polish Underground resistance. The remaining survivors were sent to death camps by the Germans. Today, 22 plaques peppered across the city mark the important buildings and borders of the Ghetto and document the existence of a rich world which formed an important part of the city's landscape before World War II.

Top of the PAST-a building

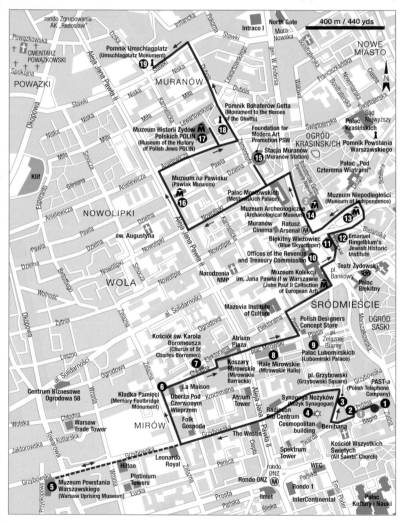

Portraits of former inhabitants of the Ghetto on the walls of an old tenement, Próżna street

PASTA

Few of Zielna Street's pre-war buildings have survived, with the exception of the former seat of the **Polish Telephone Company** ❶ (Polska Akcyjna Spółka Telefoniczna/PAST-a) – Warsaw's first skyscraper. Today, it is rather modest (51.5 metres/160ft), but in 1908 it was the tallest building in the Russian Empire. In August 1944, insurgents fought a bloody battle to take the building from the Germans, and the event is commemorated by the Polish resistance symbol visible on the roof. The famous *Kotwica* (anchor), which is a combination of the letters 'P' and 'W' ('Polska Walcząca' or 'Fighting Poland'), that you can often see on Warsaw's streets, became a symbol of the Polish underground state and the Home Army (AK). Today, PAST-a houses the Historical Education Centre and Warszawa Library, offering a wide selection of history books, map reprints, memoirs, flags and souvenirs. Just past the building, turn into Próżna street.

PRÓŻNA

In the 19th century, the majority of **Próżna street** ❷ residents were Jews, mostly traders attracted by the proximity of the city's main thoroughfare – Marszałkowska – and Grzybowski square, a dynamic ironwork centre. Before World War II the street was the beating heart of Jewish Warsaw, with well-off families occupying the tenements. Musicians, phi-lanthropists and many other prominent Jews lived on Próżna and it teemed with life until late at night. In 1940, the street was closed off by the ghetto wall.

Warsaw Uprising Museum

Since its opening in 2004, on the 60th anniversary of the outbreak of fighting, the Warsaw Uprising Museum has been one of the city's major attractions. Located in a former tram power station at Grzybowska 79, is a tribute to 'those who fought and died for independent Poland and its free capital'. It depicts not only the 63-day, uneven struggle between the Polish insurgents and their Nazi foes, but also the everyday life of civilians at the time and the post-war fate of the fighters who survived the war, but in most cases faced persecution and repression under the communist regime. Among the exhibits is a full-size replica of a Liberator B-24J bomber, weapons, documents and moving sound recordings of eyewitnesses. The highlights also include a 'sewer experience' (not for the faint-hearted); a walk in the dark sewer that Polish fighters used for communication and escape during the uprising; and a tower with fabulous views over the city and the Freedom Park at the back of the museum, where concerts are held in summer. Note that due to the harrowing nature of some exhibits, children are not allowed to see them.

Fascinating exhibits at the Warsaw Uprising Museum

Próżna remains one of the few streets in this part of the town whose historic buildings (tenements at No's 7, 9, 12 and 14) survived the ghetto destruction. In recent years, it has undergone a vast renovation, with the uncovering and cleaning of the old cobblestones, the installation of stylish lamps and pavements covered with granite flagstones. Life has gradually returned to the ground floors of the once abandoned buildings, and there are still several ironmonger's shops here. Today Próżna is the main venue of the annual **Festival of Jewish Culture Singer's Warsaw** (see page 25).

GRZYBOWSKI SQUARE

Próżna opens at the triangular **Grzybowski Square** ❸ (Plac Grzybowski), dominated by the **All Saints' Church** (Kościół Wszystkich Świętych), which, when Enrico Marconi designed it in the 19th century, was the largest church in Warsaw. The square has been recently revamped and features a pleasant, centrally located pond. Around the square are many cafés and restaurants including **Charlotte Menora**, see ❶, and Kieliszki na Próżnej. Behind the square lies the eclectic **Nożyk Synagogue** ❹ (Synagoga Nożyków) – the city's sole surviving synagogue. The 160-meter-(525ft-) tall, glass **Cosmopolitan** building (Twarda 2/4), designed by Helmut Jahn (who also designed the EU headquarters in Brussels) combines well with the architecture of the square, creating a modern and friendly space. The building attracts customers with a selection of excellent restaurants, including the first branch of Japanese chain Benihana in Poland and the Peruvian Ceviche Bar. The nearby **Polish Telecommunications Building** (TPSA) with its external panoramic lifts gliding diagonally, not vertically, is also worth a look.

From Grzybowski square, turn into Grzybowska street and walk west, passing modern hotels and Folk Gospoda restaurant. If you have at least two hours to spare, you might follow Grzybowska all the way down to reach the **Warsaw Uprising Museum** ❺ (www.1944.pl/en; Mon, Wed and Fri 8am–6pm, Thu until 8pm, Sat–Sun 10am–6pm; free on Sun; see box). Otherwise, turn right into Żelazna. Slightly further on, visible to the right between two dilapidated tenements is the exit of Krochmalna – immortalised in the short stories of the Nobel Prize-winner Isaac Bashevis Singer.

CHŁODNA

During World War II, near the junction with Żelazna, the Germans built a footbridge linking the two sections of the ghetto, which was bisected by Chłodna – at that time one of Warsaw's exit roads. When Chłodna was revitalised in 2011, a **Memory Footbridge monument** ❻ was inaugurated to commemorate this wooden footbridge that linked the so-called small and big ghettoes in 1942. On the ground floor of the corner building at Żelazna

68 is Czerwony Wieprz (Red Hog), a communist-style restaurant, with another good eatery, La Maison, behind it.

Here, turn right into Chłodna and walk until you come to the façade of the **Church of St Charles Borromeo ❼** (Kościół św. Karola Boromeusza), built from 1841 to 1849 and modelled on an early Christian basilica. The two pavilions beyond the church are remnants of the **Mirowskie Barracks** (Koszary Mirowskie), dating from 1730–32, where the royal horse guards would be stationed. Since 1851, the pavilions have been used by the fire brigade, and a small **Fire Brigade Museum** is found here.

HALE MIROWSKIE

Continue all the way down Chłodna, cross Jana Pawła II Avenue and head to **Mirowskie Halls ❽** (Hale Mirowskie; Mon–Sat 10am–7pm). Built in 1899–1901 these twin neo-romantic buildings – made of brick, with iron construction that supported the roof – were the first modern covered markets in town, with hundreds of stalls full of the most luxurious food products. They were substantially damaged during the Warsaw Uprising and had to be rebuilt after the war. The hall closer to the avenue remained a thriving bazaar. On the hall's sidewall at the junction of Mirowski Square and the avenue, you can see bullet holes in a small section of the old wall – this was where the Nazi occupiers executed over 500 Polish civilians in 1944.

Lubomirski Palace

Walking by the market halls, you reach the neo-Classical **Lubomirski Palace ❾**, now the seat of the Business Centre Club. The Palace, guarded by four lions, was turned by 78 degrees in the 1970s so that its façade would be in line with the Saxon Axis (see Route 3). On adjacent Ptasia street, at no.6, is the **Polish Designers Concept Store**, offering products by over 30 Polish clothing companies. From here turn onto Zimna (continue straight on the pavement at the end of the street), leading to Elektoralna street.

BANKOWY SQUARE

From here, follow Elektoralna to **Bankowy Square** (Plac Bankowy), whose western side is occupied by vast former government buildings, built at great expense during the era of the Congress Kingdom of the early 19th century. The domed, semicircular building at the corner of Elektoralna, designed by Antonio Corazzi in 1830, houses the **John Paul II Collection of European Art** (Kolekcja Malarstwa Europejskiego im. Jana Pawła II), donated to the Polish Church by the Porczyński family (Plac Bankowy I, closed for renovation).

The other buildings, by the same architect, include the former **Palace of the Treasury Minister** (Pałac Ministra Skarbu), and further on, the former seat of **Offices of the Revenue and Treasury Commission ❿** (Komisja Rządowa Przychodów i Skarbu), where the Polish

The Blue Skyscraper from Bankowy Square

Romantic poet Juliusz Słowacki worked as a clerk from 1829 to 1831. The monument of the poet in front of it replaced the monument of Felix Dzerzhinsky, a father of the Soviet secret police. This hated symbol of Soviet domination was eventually dismantled in 1989 to cheers from the rejoicing crowds. The second building now houses Warsaw's mayor's office.

On the other side of the square rises the **Blue Skyscraper** ⓫ (Błękitny Wieżowiec), finished in 1992, where the Great Synagogue (Wielka Synagoga) on Tłomackie Street once stood – it was destroyed by the Germans in 1943 after the Warsaw Ghetto Uprising.

THE GREAT SYNAGOGUE OF WARSAW

One of the most remarkable buildings of 19th century Warsaw, the Great Synagogue of Warsaw could seat 2,200 people and also housed a library with valuable manuscripts. Attended by acculturated Warsaw's Jewry (many sermons were in Polish), it was blown up personally by the SS-Gruppenführer Jürgen Stroop (who was in charge of quashing the Ghetto Uprising) in May 1943. You can see a model of this marvellous building at the POLIN museum (see page 78). Today, **Emanuel Ringelblum's Jewish Historic Institute** ⓬ (Żydowski Instytut Historyczny; www.jhi.pl) is at Tłomackie 3/5. Its archives comprise over 4,000 photographs documenting the Holocaust and Jewish life, while a library includes over 70,000 volumes as well as countless historic and contemporary books concerning Jewish history, culture and religion. The Institute also features a library (Księgarnia na Tłomackim; www.sforim.pl) and café.

MUSEUM OF INDEPENDENCE

From Tłomackie Street turn right into Solidarności Avenue and go east to the first zebra crossing. There, between the two lanes of the avenue is the **Museum of Independence** ⓭ (Muzeum Niepodległości; al. Solidarności 62; http://muzeum-niepodleglosci.pl; Wed–Sun 10am–5pm; free on Thu), housed in a baroque palace from the first half of the 18th century. It documents the Polish struggle for independence between the years 1914 and 1921.

ARCHAEOLOGICAL MUSEUM

Across Solidarności street, the **Archaeological Museum** ⓮ (Muzeum Archeologiczne; Długa 52, www.pma.pl; Mon–Fri 9am–4pm, Sun 10am–4pm; free on Sun) is located inside the 17th-century building of the Royal Arsenal (no.52). One side of the building faces a road, now overgrown with grass, with tram tracks set in the cobblestones: this is all that remains of **Nalewki** (now Bohaterów Getta) – the main street of Warsaw's former Jewish district. Part of the Arsenal building is occupied by the elegant **U Kucharzy**, see ❷, restaurant.

The historic fountain in front of Kino Muranów

During World War II, the Arsenal witnessed one of the Polish underground's most daring operations. On 26 March 1943, a 28-men strong elite team from Storm Groups, a Polish underground formation, attacked a German van transporting prisoners who had been interrogated at the Gestapo headquarters on Szucha street, including their troop leader Jan 'Rudy' Bytnar. The Polish fighters freed all 25 prisoners, but the badly beaten and tortured Rudy died a few days later. His interrogators were killed by the Polish underground fighters within two months.

MURANÓW

From the Arsenal, take the underground passage across Andersa Street to **Kino Muranów** (Muranów Cinema) an independent cinema with an ambitious repertoire and a historic fountain out front. Next to the cinema is the **Mostowskich Palace** (Pałac Mostowskich) a classicist building designed by Antonio Corazzi and now housing the main police station. The modern **Muranów** district was constructed after World War II on the ruins of what was the Warsaw ghetto. Its architect, Bohdan Lachert, had an ambitious project to build a new housing estate that would remind the world about the tragedy of the Jewish Warsaw. For that purpose, he reused the ruins to build new housing blocks in a modernist style. However, under pressure from the communist leader Bolesław Bierut, the idea of restoring some of the old architecture

was abandoned and socialist-realist elements were introduced to the original project. Still, Muranów remains a symbol of a long-gone world. From time to time, human remains are discovered when new buildings are under construction.

STACJA MURANÓW

Continue past the police station building, turn into Nowolipki street and then take the first street to the right, which is Zamenhofa. Continue to the junction with Dzielna street and turn right into the gateway leading to the inner courtyard. Here you will find a semi-circular building housing **Muranów Station** **⑮**

Muranów murals

When walking around Muranów (Nowolipki, Andersa, Leszno/Solidarności, Dzielna) keep your eyes peeled for murals on the buildings' walls, in the gateways or courtyards. More than a dozen of them have been created by street artists in the last few years. The Muranów murals often depict people linked with this borough or its historic Jewish culture (for example Ludwik Zamenhof, inventor of the Esperanto language, or Marek Edelman), its historic buildings (Great Synagogue) or important events. Unfortunately, the murals' lifespan is not long and many of them disappear when new buildings are constructed or the old tenements are renovated.

The bronze tree at Pawiak Museum

(Stacja Muranów) a cultural centre that organises meetings with writers, expositions, debates, workshops and guided tours around Muranów. You can get more information at the café (weekdays noon–6pm). The building also houses **Foundation for Modern Art Promotion** (PSW, Andersa 13; www.fpsw.org). Retrace your steps to Zamenhofa and continue on Dzielna.

DZIELNA

Dzielna leads to the **Pawiak Museum** 🔟 (Muzeum na Pawiaku; Dzielna 24–6, www.muzeum-niepodleglosci.pl/pawiak; Wed–Sun 10am–5pm; free on Thu). This former Tsarist prison, known as Pawiak, was a place of detention, torture and execution from 1830 until 1944, when the retreating Nazis blew it up. More than 100,000 people were processed here between 1939–44. It is estimated that 37,000 of these were executed. Following the fall of the Ghetto Uprising, the Nazis killed survivors on the streets close to the prison, while around 60,000 prisoners were sent to death camps.

Note the monument in the form of a tree (Pomnik Drzewa Pawiackiego), representing one which once stood here as a backdrop to the prisoners' suffering, and survived the destruction of the prison by the retreating Germans. Soon after the war, people started nailing small plaques with the names of their relatives killed at Pawiak to the trunk of this old elm, until it was replaced with a bronze

copy in 2004. From here, walk one block along JPII and turn right into Anielewicza street, leading to the Museum of the History of Polish Jews located at no.6.

POLIN

The **Museum of the History of Polish Jews** 🔟 also known as **POLIN** (Muzeum Historii Żydów Polskich, Mordechaja Anielewicza 6; www.polin.pl; Mon, Thu–Fri 10am–6pm, Wed, Sat–Sun 10am–8pm; the last entry two hours before closing; free on Thu) was inaugurated in 2014 and presents a 1,000-year history of Polish Jewry. Its breathtaking, award-winning building, designed by the Finnish architect Rainer Mahlamäki, boasts façades clad with copper and glass as well as panels with Hebrew and Latin letters reading 'Polin' (Hebrew for 'rest here'), the name that the first Jewish settlers, who arrived in the 13th century, gave to their new home – Poland.

The entrance, in the form of the Hebrew letter haw, hides a spectacular and symbolically charged main hall with a huge fissure between the undulating, curvy walls. The core exposition developed by 130 international scholars and displayed in eight galleries is a fascination journey through 1,000 years of history. It is a story of co-existence and cooperation, but also of rivalry and conflicts. The museum aims to celebrate life, not death, so the section dedicated to the Holocaust is comparatively small. It also wants to promote openness, tolerance and truth by hosting

POLIN *exhibit*   *Ghetto Heroes Monument detail*

concerts, workshops, film screenings and other cultural events. The museum shop has many interesting books on Jewish culture and history (also in English), plus the usual souvenirs.

TOWARDS UMSCHLAGPLATZ

In front of the museum, there is a huge square, in the middle of which stands a **Monument to the Heroes of the Ghetto** ⑱ (Pomnik Bohaterów Getta). This highly expressive work was unveiled in 1948 amidst a sea of ruins. It is made entirely of labradorite, which the Nazis had imported from Sweden with the aim of creating monuments to the antici-pated victory of the Reich. The monu-ment made headlines when the German Chancellor Willy Brandt knelt here as a gesture of reconciliation in 1970. Nearby is a monument of Jan Karski sitting on a bench. He was a Polish resistance fighter and a famous courier from Warsaw, who reported to the Polish government in exile and the Western Allies on the Nazi atrocities in occupied Poland, including the extermination of the Jews.

The monument to the Heroes of the Ghetto marks the starting point of **the Jewish Martyrdom Memorial Trail** (Trakt Pamięci Męczenstwa i Walki Żyd-ów), created in 1988. It consists of 16 blocks of grey granite commemorating the several hundred thousand Jews mur-dered by the Nazis in the Warsaw Ghetto and death camps. The trail ends at the **Umschlagplatz Monument** ⑲ (Pom-

nik Umschlagplatz), formerly a railway siding, situated at the corner of Dzika and Stawki streets. It was here that the Germans rounded up thousands of Jews from the ghetto in order to trans-port them in cattle wagons to the death camp at Treblinka. You can end the walk here or continue along Dzika to reach the Radosław roundabout with a huge Pol-ish flag in the centre, from where you can take a tram to the city centre.

Food and drink

❶ CHARLOTTE MENORA
Pl. Grzybowski; tel: 0 668 669 137; http://bistrocharlotte.pl; Mon–Thu 7am–midnight, Fri 7am–1am, Sat 9am–1am, Sun 9am–10pm (til midnight in summer); €
Just like its first bistro at Zbawiciela Square (see page 120) the bread is baked on the premises, but the menu is enriched with Jewish staples including bagels, challah and *caviar juif* (chopped liver). The garden is beautifully located for the summer.

❷ U KUCHARZY
Długa 55, Arsenal; tel. 022 826 79 36; www.gessler.pl; daily noon–last customer; €€€–€€€€
This restaurant has a spacious, modern interior and the open kitchen in the middle is famous for its fresh steak tartare, prepared in front of the customer. Offers a good value set lunch with two options: meat or vegetarian.

The Palace Of Culture

FROM PALACE OF CULTURE TO KONSTYTUCJI SQUARE

This diverse route covers the relics of Warsaw's communist past, including the monumental Palace of Culture, as well as dazzling shrines to hedonism where the city's beautiful people flock to party their nights away.

DISTANCE: 4.5km (14.7 miles)
TIME: Half a day
START: Palace of Culture
END: Konstytucji Square
POINTS TO NOTE: Try to end this route in the early evening when the bars and pubs at Constitution Square and Koszyki market really get going.

Visitors often complain that unlike any other large cities in Europe, Warsaw lacks a centre. The huge area around the Palace of Culture, swept by chilly winds in autumn and winter, seems awkward as the heart of the city. This is partly because the legal status of land adjacent to the Palace of Culture was uncertain for a long time. After World War II, the communist authorities nationalised all land in the city and took over buildings that survived the war. The lengthy reprivatisation process begun after the restoration of democracy in 1989 has dragged on for decades and had its fair share of scandals in which high-ranking city officials were involved. As a result, plans concerning this part of town are vague and subject to constant changes.

PALACE OF CULTURE AND SCIENCE

Varsovians have ambivalent feelings about **The Palace of Culture ❶** (Pałac Kultury, www.pkin.pl), the city's highest building and a personal 'gift' of Joseph Stalin, built between 1952–55. Even now, over 60 years later, some still believe it to be a symbol of Soviet domination and would rather see it demolished. But the majority of Varsovians have got used to its familiar, bulky form and can't imagine the city without it. The Palace is a gem of Socialist-realism architecture and inscribed on the list of protected heritage buildings. On the outside, the palace is guarded by several huge classical sculptures including that of the Polish astronomer and mathematician Copernicus, the Romantic poet Adam Mickiewicz and the physicist Marie Curie, as well as model socialist workers. The lavish interior contains more than 3,000 rooms and dazzles visitors with elegant marble floors, weighty glass chandeliers,

View from the terrace   Ormate interiors at the Palace of Culture

furniture and lamps designed by the best Polish artists and craftsmen. According to many, the palace's interior is effectively a museum of Polish applied arts from the early 1950s.

Viewing terrace

From the beginning, the palace was a multifunctional building; it now houses offices, cultural institutions, two concert halls, a private university, a post office,

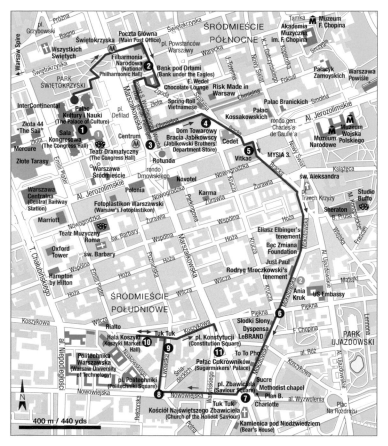

The Congress Hall

cinema, theatres and a swimming pool. Nevertheless, its biggest draw remains the large **Viewing Terrace** (www.pkin.pl/strefa-turysty-taras-widokowy, daily 10am–8pm, in summer also Fri–Sat 8–11.30pm). Two ultra-fast lifts whizz tourists to the observation deck in a matter of seconds. It is located about 114 meters (374ft) above the ground on the 30th floor and offers astonishing panoramic views over surrounding buildings including the Złote Tarasy shopping centre next to the **Central Railway Station**, and several skyscrapers constructed in recent years. This includes the **Warsaw Spire** (220 metres/722ft), **Q22**, the highest office building in town, designed by the Polish architecture firm Kuryłowicz & Associates, and the 192-metre-(630ft-) tall **Złota 44**, popularly known as 'The Sail', designed by world-famous architect Daniel Libeskind. The 30th floor of the palace also features the **Gothic Room**, home to impressive rib vaults and exquisite floors, comprising an in-house gallery and café. Another popular attraction is a virtual reality application called 'History Horizon', that allows visitors to see Warsaw as it was in the 11th, 14th and 16th centuries, and just after the 1944 uprising.

The Congress Hall

The palace also features the **Sala Kongresowa** (the Congress Hall; currently under renovation), once the venue of communist party leadership rallies as well as famous concerts, including a legend-ary performance by the Rolling Stones in 1967 (one of the first concerts behind the Iron Curtain by the group) which triggered riots in and outside the hall. Trendy **Cafe Kulturalna**, see ❶, located on the ground level next to the **Teatr Dramatyczny** (Theatre), is a perfect place for a short refuelling stop or lunch.

JASNA STREET

Exit the Palace of Culture and head left towards the beautifully revamped Świętokrzyska street, lined with trees and featuring wide pavements with cycling paths. Head east, crossing a busy intersection with Marszałkowska street and turn right into Jasna street. Continue past the **Main Post Office** (Poczta Główna) building to reach the **National Philharmonic Hall ❷** (Filharmonia Narodowa; http://filharmonia.pl) at No 5, which has been here since 1901. The building was once the pride of Warsaw, astonishing visitors with the richness of its decoration. After World War II, it was rebuilt in a simplified, Socialist-realist form. First-rate orchestras play here on a regular basis, and every five years the building hosts the world-renowned Chopin Piano Competition. Slightly further on at No 1 rises the monumental **Bank under the Eagles** (Bank pod Orłami), whose name derives from the façade's two stone eagles; the building, designed by Jan Heurich the Younger and completed in 1915, is a pioneering work of modern Polish architecture.

Jabłkowski Brothers' Department Store

PASAŻ WIECHA AND CHMIELNA

Turn right into Złota and then left into the **Pasaż Stefana Wiecheckiego 'Wiecha'** ❸ (the 'Wiech' passage), a pedestrianised alleyway located at the back of the department stores lining Marszałkowska street. Formerly known as Domy Towarowe Centrum, these were state-owned until the fall of communism. Privatised after 1989, they now feature international chain stores including H&M, C&A, Zara, Apple and TK Maxx.

Once the city's main shopping street, Chmielna now features nicely renovated buildings with charming courtyards. The house at no. 30 dates from 1906 and is the only example in Warsaw to be influenced by the so-called Zakopane style, recalling the wooden architecture of the Polish highlands. Continue on Chmielna to the corner of Zgoda, Szpitalna and Bracka streets. If you need a break, make a short detour to the nearby Wedel chocolate parlour on Szpitalna street (at no.8), passing Spring Roll Vietnamese restaurant and Risk Made in Warsaw (www.risk madeinwarsaw.com) at no 6 (in the courtyard), owned by two Polish female designers, selling comfortable clothes made of top-quality sweatshirt cotton.

BRACKA STREET

Opened in 1914, the **Jabłkowski Brothers' Department Store** ❹ (Dom Towarowy Bracia Jabłkowscy) at Bracka 25, was the first large department store in

Warsaw, and its interior features a huge Post-Secessionist stained-glass window. The children's department store Smyk used to stand across the street. Built in a late modernist style, it was heavily criticised by representatives of the socialist-realist school as being too 'cosmopolitan'. Its demolition caused widespread protests, but the new building, **Cedet**, will resemble the original.

Continue on Bracka and cross Jerozolimskie Avenue to start the quintes-

Fotoplastikon

From the Palace of Culture you can make a short detour to see Warsaw's Fotoplastikon (Fotoplastikon Warszawski, http://fotoplastikonwarszawski.pl; Aleje Jerozolimskie 51, Wed–Sun 10am–6pm). Fotoplastikons (also called Kaiser panoramas) were invented in Germany in the second half of 19th century and became extremely popular in Europe over the next few decades, presenting 3D photographs from across the world. The Warsaw one dates back from 1905 and is one of the few still in operation. Supposedly, it was used as a contact point for the Polish underground during World War II. Now it offers regular shows that last about 20 minutes, a genuine journey back in time. Every Sunday, a collection of Warsaw photographs taken at the turn of the 19th century is shown. The Fotoplastikon also hosts cultural workshops for children called 'Lazy Sunday' (every Sun at 11am).

Louis Vuitton at Vitkac

sential Warsaw shopping trip. At Bracka no 9 is a monumental black granite building designed by Stefan Kuryłowicz. **Vitkac ❺** (www.vitkac.com) is the poshest and most expensive of all city's shopping meccas, with boutiques for sought-after designers including Louis Vuitton.

Off Bracka lies the short Mysia street with another elegant, but much smaller, department store at no.3 (www.mysia3.pl). It boasts the first branch of COS in Poland, the She is a Riot concept store and Orska Jewellery, as well as Muji and Nap outlets. After bargain hunting, head to Leica's Photography Gallery located on the top floor. Bracka ends at the **Trzech Krzyży square** (see page 56) with more fashion boutiques. Walk along the square, making sure the church is on your left, and enter **Mokotowska street ❻**.

MOKOTOWSKA STREET

This elegant street has retained some of its pre-war Warsaw charm. Completed in 1904, **Eliasz Elbinger's tenement** at no.65 surprisingly survived the war unscathed. Another interesting building is **Rodryg Mroczkowski's tenement** at no.57. Dating from 1904, it features 'Krakowiacy i Górale' (Cracovians and Highlanders) figures in folk costumes which support the balconies. An eclectic tenement at no.50 was where Józef Piłsudski, one of the architects of Poland's independence after World War I, once lived. Other houses worth a look on Mokotowska include a low tenement at no.48 built in 1860, a beautiful pastel blue house at no.41, the **Pałac Cukrowników** (Sugarmakers' Palace) at no.25 and the **Kamienica pod Niedźwiedziem** (Bear's House) at no.8.

Fashion galore

Mokotowska is also a favourite street of young Polish designers. At no.61 is Ania Kuczyńska's boutique. One of the most distinguished fashion designers in the country, she was called a 'pole star' by *Wallpaper* magazine. Her style is often described as 'ornate minimalism'. Located at no.52 is Loft37 (https://loft37.eu), where it is possible to design your own shoes. Meanwhile, pricey streetwear by Robert Kupisz is sold at Mokotowska 48. Other boutiques worth popping in include Ania Kruk (no.46), Just Paul (no.61) and Le Brand (no.39).

Top-class designers attract a clientele with a huge appetite not only for modern fashion but also for fine cuisine. Mokotowska does not disappoint and has something to suit every taste and pocket. From the widely acclaimed **Ale Wino**, see ❷, restaurant to the cheap but tasty To To Pho Vietnamese eatery, there is no need to explore Mokotowska with an empty stomach. Don't forget about dessert – hand-made ice cream at Sucre (no 12) is delicious.

PLAC ZBAWICIELA

At the end of Mokotowska lies trendy **Plac Zbawiciela ❼** (Saviour Square), a favour-

Mokotowska street detail   *Koszyki Market Hall*

ite meeting point for the town's young bohemians. Situated at the confluence of three large streets: Marszałkowska, Mokotowska and Nowowiejska, it was named after the church dominating the square. The **Church of the Holiest Saviour** (Kościół Najświętszego Zbawiciela) was consecrated in 1927 but bears resemblance to the Polish Renaissance and baroque periods. Meanwhile, the circular plaza itself was designed in the 18th century by architect Jan Chrystian Schuch. Today, it is lined with popular cafés and eateries including the iconic Charlotte, which is always crowded with hipsters sipping lattes, beer or wine and the club Plan B. Opposite is the equally popular Karma and Tuk Tuk, offering authentic Thai street food. The square gets very lively at night. Before 1914, the house at no 12 was the tallest building in Warsaw. For many decades it has housed a Methodist chapel and English language school run by the Methodists.

WARSAW UNIVERSITY OF TECHNOLOGY

Leave the square by taking Nowowiejska street, which opens up onto **Politechniki Square** ❽ with a small roundabout in the centre. The main building of the **Warsaw University of Technology** (also known as Polytechnic) is behind it. Built at the turn of the 19th century, it features a grand hall where different events and balls are held. Turn right into **Lwowska street** ❾, featuring many houses from the beginning of the 20th century, some of which have been spectacularly renovated. Fortunately, the street did not suffer major damage during World War II and still oozes a pre-war charm. The oldest house on Lwowska (at no 9) dates back from 1905. At the end of the street turn left into Koszykowa, leading to the newest attraction in this part of town.

HALA KOSZYKI

Built in 1906–8, the **Koszyki Market Hall** ❿ (Hala Koszyki; www.koszyki.com; Mon–Sat 8am–1am; Sun from 9am) was designed in an Art Nouveau style by Juliusz Dzierżanowski. At that time, it was a very modern market with electric refrigerators and tiled pools for the living fish. Each stand was meticulously designed. During the Warsaw Uprising the hall was burnt down and largely destroyed. Rebuilt after the war, it was taken over by a state-owned Społem company, but slid into ruin in the first decade of the 21st century. It wasn't reopened until 2016, following incredible revitalisation carried out by architects from JEMS Architekci studio, who renovated the original steel construction and reused the original tiles and other details to create a modern food court and social centre. Teeming with life day or night, Koszyki boasts dozens of restaurants, shops, a supermarket, art gallery and exhibition spaces as well as a culinary academy.

Leave the market hall and follow Koszykowa street to Konstytucji Square.

Plac Konstytucji

MDM

A socialist realism flagship project, the **Marszałkowska Housing Estate** (Marszałkowska Dzielnica Mieszkaniowa; MDM) was the brainchild of architects Józef Sigalin and Stanisław Jankowski. The huge housing complex was built in 1950–52 and inscribed in the register of heritage monuments in 2015. To make space for the new development, numerous old tenements that survived the war had to be demolished in the area stretching from Unii Lubelskiej Square to Jerozolimskie Avenue.

The heart of the MDM is the rectangular **Plac Konstytucji** ⓫ (Constitution Square) surrounded by massive housing blocks with arcades hiding shops, restaurants and cafés. The square was meant to be a symbol of new power and its ideology. Paradoxically, the huge blocks surrounding it were modelled, as far as their form was concerned, after the 'capitalist and aristocratic' architecture of the house at Małachowskiego square (at no 2) which once belonged to the noble Krasińscy family. The northern side of the square features two identical buildings with reliefs representing the architects, engineers and workers who built MDM. Look out for three gigantic candelabras standing at the southern end of the square. Contrary to posterior housing estates built by the communist governments, no expense was spared either on materials (which included sandstone and granite) or on advanced technologies. However, the funds quickly dried up and other projects linked to the MDM development were not half as grand. Moreover, Stalin's death in 1953 marked the symbolic end of Socialist realism.

Food and drink

① **CAFÉ KULTURALNA**
Pl. Defilad 1; tel: 22 656 62 81;
www.kulturalna.pl; daily noon–last customer; €€
As the name suggests, this is a very 'cultural' café located next to the Dramatic Theatre attracting a mostly highbrow crowd. The menu is short and no-nonsense, including a handful of starters, three soups and a modest selection of main dishes. But the food is not that important as long as the vibe is good and the party gets going.

② **ALE WINO!**
Mokotowska 48, tel: 022 628 38 30;
www.alewino.pl; Mon 5–11pm, Tue–Sat noon–11pm; €€–€€€€
The key to success here has been a perfect combination of the best wines, delicious food, perfect service and relaxed atmosphere. Few restaurants in town could pulled this off, but Ale Wino has passed the test with flying colours. Creative chef Sebastian Wełpa has a flair for distinctive dishes such as celeric ravioli and cauliflower or risotto with skrei & yakiniku sauce. Booking advisable.

Wilanów's opulent interior

WILANÓW

The summer palace of King Jan III Sobieski, the vanquisher of the Turks, is known as 'the Polish Versailles'. Its elegant, manicured gardens and equally beautiful 'wild' park by the canal are perfect for strolling in.

DISTANCE: 2.6km (1.6 miles)
TIME: 4 hours
START: Wilanów cemetery
END: Temple of Divine Providence
POINTS TO NOTE: Wilanów can be easily reached from the city centre by bus (180, 116 and 519) – get off at the Wilanów stop.

The charming Wilanów palace was once the private summer retreat of King Jan III Sobieski. Originally a manor house, it was eventually transformed into a huge stately residence named 'Villa Nova', which was 'translated' into Wilanów. It is the last stop on the 6km (3.7-mile) Royal Route. Construction of Jan III Sobieski's summer residence began in 1677, with a great number of fine artists involved in the project. Contrary to most parts of the city, it survived the war almost unscathed, although it was looted by the Germans. Today, the palace accommodates a museum, where you can see well-preserved rooms dating from Sobieski's time, as well as the Polish Portrait Gallery.

AROUND THE PALACE

Next to the bus terminus lies a scenic **cemetery ❶** dating from the 19th century, where you can find tombs of the 1863 insurgents, 1939 soldiers and Polish resistance fighters killed during the 1944 Warsaw Uprising. Leaving the cemetery, cross the multi-lane Przyczółkowa street. On the left is the restaurant **Kuźnia Kulturalna**, see ❶, housed in the former 18th-century smithy. It is also known for regular concerts and poetry slams.

After turning into the cobbled Stanisława Kostki Potockiego street, you will see a restaurant called Wilanów on your right. In the 1970's it was said to be the smartest in communist Poland.

The **Church of St Anne ❷** (Kościół św. Anny), rebuilt in 1857–1870 by the famous architect Henryk Marconi, contains several tomb slabs marking the last owners of Wilanów – the Potocki and Branicki families. Inside, on the first pillar on the right is a mammoth's bone, found when the foundations of the church were laid in 1770.

When you exit the church, you will

pass through the forecourt, now a park, in which the neo-Gothic **mausoleum of Stanislaw Kostka Potocki** ❸ stands; he was a former owner of Wilanów and a connoisseur of antiquities. It was Potocki who, in 1805, set up a museum in the palace and opened its doors to the public; he also remodelled the gardens as an English-style landscaped park. His equestrian portrait by Jacques-Louis David can be seen in the palace's museum.

To the right, on Stanistawa Kostki Potockiego street at no.10/16, is the **Poster Museum** (Muzeum Plakatu; www. postermuseum.pl; Mon noon–4pm, Tue, Thu and Fri 10am–4pm, Wed, Sat and Sun until 6pm; free on Mon) inside a 19th-century coach house. It holds over 60,000 Polish and international posters.

WILANÓW PALACE

Pass through the entrance gate, dating from Sobieski's time, which is crowned with two allegorical figures representing War and Peace. At the far end of the courtyard, the palace is surrounded by long outbuildings. Its façade is adorned with sculptural decorations glorifying the majesty of Sobieski; some allude to his

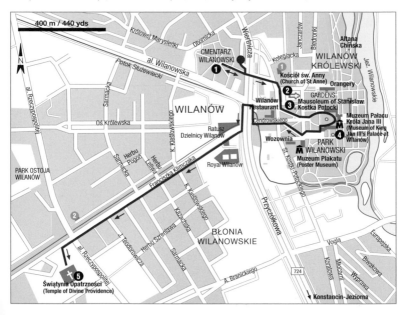

Wilanów Palace

military victories, others pay tribute, by means of allegory, to the virtues of the king and his wife Queen Marysieńka. Since the beginning of 21st century, the palace and surrounding gardens have been undergoing revitalisation aimed at restoring its original baroque style.

The museum

Today, the palace accommodates the **Museum of King Jan III's Palace at Wilanów ❹** (Muzeum Pałacu Króla Jana III w Wilanowie; www.wilanow-palac.pl; Apr–mid Oct Wed and Sat–Mon 9.30am–6pm, Tue, Thu–Fri 9.30am–4pm, mid Oct–Mar daily except Tue 9.30am–4pm, park from 9am to Oct–Mar 4pm, Sep–Oct 7pm, Apr 8pm, Aug and May 9pm, Jun–Jul 10pm; free on Thu) consisting of two sections. The lower floor comprises royal apartments while the upper one (closed to the public at the time of writing) is occupied by the **Gallery of the Polish**, with effigies of Polish monarchs, noblemen, patriots and artists accumulated over the centuries. Of particular interest are the valuable coffin portraits from the 17th century.

However, the museum's biggest attraction are the **royal apartments** of King Sobieski and Queen Maria Kazimiera, dating back to 1677–96. The bed in the royal bedchamber is decorated with Turkish fabrics captured by Sobieski during the siege of Vienna, while the walls and ceilings are covered with 17th-century allegorical paintings. In the southern wing, a major attraction is the **apartment of Princess Izabela**

Lubomirska, who inherited the palace in 1771; it features a private **bathhouse** (Pawilon kąpielowy). The northern wing,

Jan III Sobieski

Born in 1629 in Olesko, near Lwów (now Lviv in Ukraine) to a Polish-Lithuanian family, Sobieski became one of the most admired and popular kings in Poland's history. Having been educated in philosophy at the Jagiellonian University in Kraków, he spent time travelling Western Europe, visiting Paris, London and The Hague. The future king mingled with European monarchs and aristocrats, and mastered three languages: French, German and Italian (he already knew Latin). Following his return home, he distinguished himself in battles with Cossacks and Tatars during the Khmelnytsky Uprising. As royal envoy to Constantinople in the Ottoman Empire, Sobieski studied Turkish military traditions and learnt Turkish as well as Tartar. He honed his commander skills during the Swedish Deluge, becoming the King of the Polish and Lithuanian Commonwealth in 1674. His most famous victory came in 1683 at the Vienna Battle, when Sobieski defeated the Turkish army under Kara Mustafa and was hailed as a 'Saviour of Vienna and the Western Civilisation'. He was married to his beloved French wife Marie Casimire Louise ('Marysieńka' in Poland), to whom he wrote passionate letters regarded as masterpieces of Polish epistolography.

The Temple of Divine Providence

in turn, has 19th-century interiors arranged by Potocki; the highlight is the **Great Crimson Room** (Wielki Pokój Karmazynowy), where, on occasion, official receptions were held for visiting heads-of-state. Other rooms worth mentioning are the sumptuous **White Hall**, with huge wall mirrors, and the **Etruscan Cabinet**, housing a unique collection of ancient amphorae bought or personally excavated by Stanisław Kostka Potocki at Nola near Naples at the end of the 18th century.

Gardens

The gardens' central section comprises a formal baroque park in the French-Italian style. Points of interest here are a sundial from 1684 with a sculpture of Chronos, the god of time, 19th-century Romantic buildings, and an 18th-century orangery housing a display of handicrafts.

TEMPLE OF DIVINE PROVIDENCE

Across from the palace, on the other side of Przyczółkowa, rise the new Wilanów housing estates. Where cabbages and carrots grew only a decade ago now stand elegant housing blocks plus cafés, restaurants and the gigantic **Temple of Divine Providence** ❻ (Świątynia Opatrzności), referred to as a huge citrus squeezer by its critics. Located at the end of Klimczaka street, its history goes back to 1791 when the parliament passed a resolution to construct the temple as a symbol of grati-tude for the 3rd of May Constitution. The idea was revived after Poland regained its independence in 1918, but it did not come to its fruition because of the war. Finally, it was inaugurated in 2016. The complex includes the church, a **Museum of John Paul II and Primate Stefan Wyszyński**, and a **Pantheon of Great Poles**.

Across the street from the temple is **Vilanova Wilanów**, see ❷, where you can refuel after visiting the complex.

Food and drink

❶ KUŹNIA KULTURALNA

Kostki Potockiego 24; tel: 500 200 200; www.kuzniakulturalna.pl; daily 11am–10pm; €€–€€€

Known for its cultural events, this restaurant is conveniently located next to the Church of St Anne and has a pleasant front garden. The menu is a mix of Polish (pierogi, liver, grilled ribs) and international dishes (pastas, steaks and tuna).

❷ VILANOVA WILANÓW

Klimczaka 22; tel: 022 412 04 57; http://vilanova.pl; Mon–Sat noon–11pm, Sun until 10pm; €€€

This modern restaurant offers good-value set lunch menus for 22zł from Monday to Friday. Items ordered á la carte are more expensive and include grilled beef loin steak (74zł) and roast duck. The restaurant features a separate children's play area.

St Florian Church

OLD PRAGA

For a long time Praga was regarded as the 'worse' part of the city. Today it is experiencing unprecedented revival and gentrification with historic townhouses and post-industrial estates being renovated and converted into art galleries, museums, trendy clubs and shops.

DISTANCE: 4.7km (3 miles)
TIME: Three hours
START: Park Praski
END: Salesian Basilica of the Holy Heart of Jesus
POINTS TO NOTE: The easiest way to reach Park Praski is take tram 4, 13, 23 or 26 from Bankowy Square or the Old Town. This tour can be easily combined with Route 12 or 14.

It wasn't until the late 18th century that Warsaw's right-bank, known as Praga, was incorporated into the capital. It was an area where Catholicism, Orthodoxy and Judaism peacefully co-existed and which largely escaped the devastation of World War II.

The first villages on this side of the river emerged in the 12–13th century on land originally covered by forest. In 1648, King Władysław IV granted Praga a city charter, but it wasn't until 1791 that it was incorporated into Warsaw. Three years later, during the Kościuszko Uprising, Praga was devastated by a storming Russian army led by General Aleksandr Suvorov. After the battle, Russian soldiers slaughtered up to 20,000 civilians. Then it was turn of the French allies under Napoleon to demolish more than 200 buildings between 1807–8 to clear space for the planned fortifications. The second half of the 19th century saw a rapid industrialisation of Praga triggered by the completion of the permanent Kierbedzia Bridge over Vistula in 1869, and construction of new railway lines.

The borough has experienced dramatic changes in recent years. The main thoroughfare Targowa has been modernised, with a second metro line reaching the Wileński railway station and a posh housing estate has sprung up next to Port Praski.

ST FLORIAN CHURCH

Across the bustling Solidarności Avenue, just opposite Praski Park, stands the imposing neo-Gothic **St Florian Church** ❶ (Kościół Świętego Floriana), completed in 1904. It was designed by Józef Pius Dziekoński, who wanted to give the

church a characteristic Polish Gothic form, whilst at the same time modelling it on French cathedrals and the churches of Western Pomerania. The twin towers were deliberately designed to be taller than the cupola of the nearby Orthodox church in order to prove that Warsaw was still a Polish, western city, and not a Russian, eastern one. The church was blown up by the Nazis in 1944, and rebuilt after the war in a slightly simplified form. A large, crescent-like building west to the church is the **Praski Hospital** (Szpital Praski), established in 1868.

FLORIAŃSKA STREET

On leaving the church, proceed along Floriańska street, noting fragments of the cobbled road, historic street lamps and a large building known as the **Brzozowski Tenement** (Kamienica Brzozowskiego) at no.8, dating from 1911–12. A modern vis-a-vis townhouse at no. 6 houses **Gosia Baczyńska Atelier** (Mon–Fri 11am–7pm, Sat noon–3pm; www.gosia baczynska.com), a boutique of the successful Polish designer. The building on Floriańska 2 was built for widows of Russian soldiers. In 1924 it served as a house for the January Uprising's veterans. Today it is used by the Warsaw-Prague diocese's curia.

On the small square at the corner of Floriańska and Kłopotowskiego stands the **Monument to the Praga Courtyard Band ②** (Pomnik Praskiej Kapeli Podwórkowej) dedicated to a famous pre-war

local band. Similar street bands used to be a popular sight on the streets of the occupied Warsaw; their songs lifted the spirits and encouraged resistance.

From here, you may turn right onto Kłopotowskiego street to reach a former **Customs House ③** (Dawna Komora Wodna) at no1/3. Standing close to the river bank, it is one of the most valuable

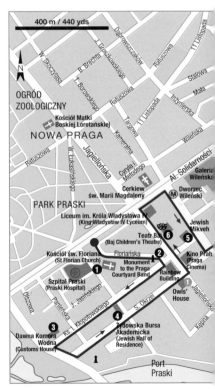

Monument to the Praga Courtyard Band

and oldest historic buildings in Praga, designed by Antonio Corazzi in 1824–25. It was located at the entry of the old bridge which no longer exists and served as toll collection point. The building is decorated with a relief by Tomasz Accardi showing Neptune, God of the seas, riding a chariot pulled by horses with fish tails and surrounded by dolphins.

Follow Kłopotowskiego to the traffic lights and turn left. Walk along the river for about 100 metres (328ft) and turn into Stefana Okrzei street.

OKRZEI STREET

To the right is **Praga Port Development**, an award-winning office and apartment

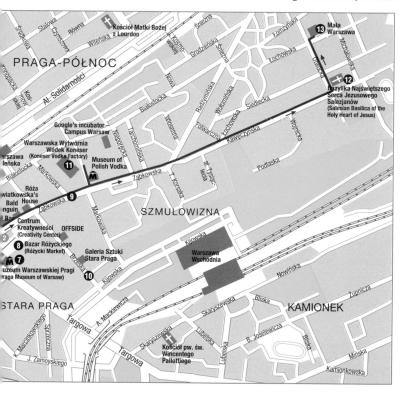

Różycki Market sells an extraordinary range of wares

complex built around the old Praga port which operated until the 1960s, and the former abattoir on Krowia street ('Cow street'). Follow Okrzei to the corner of Sierakowskiego and turn left. At no 7, is a former **Jewish Hall of Residence** ❹ (Żydowska Bursa Akademicka), a large, neo-baroque building. After World War II, the communist secret police used the cellars of the building as torture cells. Back on Okrzei, it is worth taking a quick look at the restored **corner tenement** at no. 26, 'Owls' House', whose flaking facade is adorned with owls, griffins and bats. It was built in 1906 for Prince Bronisław Massalski. On the ground floor is a hip club/café called **Centrum Zarządzania Światem** (The World Management Centre), see ❶, a good place for lunch or having fun at regular cultural events.

JAGIELLOŃSKA STREET

Next, turn left into Jagiellońska. On the right you will find the **Kino Praha** (Praga Cinema) with reliefs of famous Polish actors, while on the left side of the street stands the so-called **Tęczowy Budynek** (Rainbow Building) a former department store completed in 1952, which now houses revenue office.

A short detour to Kłopotowskiego street will lead you to the former **Jewish Mikveh** ❺ (a bath used for ritual immersions in Judaism; Mykwa) building at no. 31. Owned by the Jewish Community of Warsaw, this red-brick house

– completed in 1914 – is now the seat of the Multicultural Lyceum named after Jacek Kuroń, one of the key figures of the democratic opposition movement during communist times, and a labour and social policy minister after fall of the communism in 1989. Next to the lyceum is a small square where the Praga Synagogue stood until 1961, when it was demolished. All that is left are the fundaments and a small mound. A reconstruction of the synagogue is now being considered.

Back on Jagiellońska, note a building at no.28 crowned with a striking gable in Polish Renaissance and baroque style. This is the **Baj Children's Theatre** ❻ (Teatr dla najmłodszych Baj; http://teatr baj.pl), which occupies a former Jewish Children's Home founded by trader and philanthropist Michał Bergson. Designed in 1914 by Stifelman and Weiss, the building's façade features decor based on Jewish themes.

Next to it is the **King Władysław IV Lyceum** (Liceum im. Króla Władysława IV), the most prestigious of the Praga high schools and alma mater of famous people such as Janusz Korczak (see box).

A revitalised Minter's tenement from 1867 at no.56 is home to **Centrum Kreatywności** (Creativity Center), an entrepreneurship incubator for start-ups and a technical and institutional support centre. The most important part of the centre is the creative working area, meant to encourage development of innovative ideas in design, fashion, games, architecture, film, video and music.

Ząbkowska street

PRAGA MUSEUM OF WARSAW

You can learn about the history of Praga at the small but interesting **Praga Museum of Warsaw** ❼ (Muzeum Warszawskiej Pragi; Targowa 50/52; http://muzeumpragi.pl; Tue–Wed and Fri–Sun 10am–6pm, Thu until 8pm; free on Thu). The museum has a unique feature: it was created in close collaboration with the local community, which remains involved in the museum's activities. The museum is spread over two floors and not overloaded with exhibits. A nice little café, Niebieski Syfon, serves excellent *pyzy*, craft beers and delicious cakes.

RÓŻYCKI MARKET

Framed by Targowa, Ząbkowska and Brzeska streets, the **Różycki Market** ❽ has certainly seen better days. Yet, in spite of its decline, the place is still full of local character. It was founded at the end of 19th century by Julian Różycki, owner of several pharmacies, and it was meant to be Praga's commercial centre. During World War II it operated as a black market, where normally inaccessible products from German military warehouses – from weapons to food – could be bought. After the war, the market flourished as official shops, always struggling with shortages, had little to offer. Meanwhile at Różycki Market one could buy virtually anything: from US dollars and other Western currencies,

jeans and bubble gum smuggled over the border, to chickens and the famous *pyzy* (potato dumplings) in jars.

ZĄBKOWSKA STREET

Leaving the market, it is worth taking a walk on **Ząbkowska** ❾. This street, very neglected until recently, has been completely transformed over the past few years, with artists moving in and opening ateliers and galleries. On special weekends, the street is closed to traffic, which attracts even more people from across the river. Slowly but surely, Ząbkowska's sketchy reputation is slipping into oblivion. It is now definitely a major tourist attraction on this side of the river. A landmark at the corner of Targowa is *Praskie Aniołki* (Praga's Angels) is a group of sculptured fairytale figures crafted by

Janusz Korczak

Janusz Korczak was a Jewish-Polish educator, pediatrician and children's writer. During World War II he was also director of the orphanage for Jewish children, whom he refused to abandon; first when they were moved to the Warsaw Ghetto and again in 1942 when the Germans sent almost 200 of them to the extermination camp at Treblinka. Korczak went with them, declining various offers to be smuggled out of the Ghetto by the Polish underground. He and his children most probably died in Treblinka in a gas chamber.

Enjoying a drink at W Oparach Absurdu café

Marek Sułek, which refers to the local belief in guardian angels. In winter, each of the angels gets a custom-made outfit, probably so as not to catch a cold.

Ząbkowska is also known for its historic shrines, usually hidden away in the backyards or in the gates. There are more than 100 of them. They appeared during German occupation and the Warsaw Uprising as a replacement for destroyed churches. A particularly valuable shrine showing the Madonna and Child sculpted in stone can be found at the corner of Ząbkowska and Korsaka streets.

There are plenty of eateries and drinking holes on Ząbkowska, so you won't go hungry or thirsty whilst walking along it. Bar Ząbkowski near the junction with Targowa has been here for half a century. It offers *pierogi* and *pyzy* as well as good-value lunch menus. A good alternative is the classic bar, **W Oparach Absurdu**, see ❷ (In the Fumes of Absurdity), at no.6. This watering hole has an original interior with plenty of old furniture. On the menu are regional beers, liquors and spirits.

The courtyard of the tenement at no.13 (Dom Róży Kwiatkowskiej/Róża Kwiatkowska's House) has a preserved wooden gallery leading to the apartments and recalls the narrow passageways and crowded atmosphere of small Jewish towns in the former Polish-Lithuanian Commonwealth. In the same building, facing the street, is the Caffee and Bistro Galeria Sztuki (www.caffee.stanowski.pl) an interesting blend of café/restaurant and old furniture gallery (it can be bought here). Another store belonging to the same owner, Galeria Sztuki Stara Praga, can be found on Brzeska 6.

Altogether different is the house at Ząbkowska no.11, where you can sit in the Łysy Pingwin (Bald Penguin) bar and listen to soul music. This pub and art gallery attracts artists and organises concerts and exhibitions.

BRZESKA

Ząbkowska intersects with **Brzeska street** ❿ – the stretch to the right of ul. Ząbkowska used to be considered one of the most dangerous places in Warsaw. During communist times, almost every house here was an illegal *melina*, where you could buy alcohol. Today, you should still take care in this area, only visiting it in the daylight and watching your belongings – although it is probably no more dangerous than parts of New York or London. On Brzeska you might consider visiting OFFSIDE club and Pyzy Flaki Gorące restaurant offering Praga's staples: tripe soup (*flaczki*) and *pyzy*. In the courtyard of the house at no.9 is yet another shrine from the German occupation period.

If you need a caffeine shot, head to Mucha nie siada, a café with excellent Italian coffee served in a thousand ways (at least that's what they claim), drinks at bargain prices and plenty to eat, too.

The large complex of brick buildings comprising the **Koneser Vodka Factory** ⓫ (Warszawska Wytwórnia

Brzeska tenements   Koneser Vodka Factory

Wódek Koneser) is entered through a decorative gate that looks like a miniature medieval castle. Millions of litres of vodka have been produced here since 1897. Work is underway to create the **Museum of Polish Vodka** here to 'promote history and the unique character of the Polish national drink'. One of the factory buildings on the premises occupies Google's incubator – Campus Warsaw.

After the junction with Radzymińska street, Ząbkowska merges with Kawęczyńska street. To the right, you pass an old tram terminus composed of striking – albeit neglected – buildings, and after a few minutes you reach a square dominated by the monumental **Salesian Basilica of the Holy Heart of Jesus** ⓬ (Bazylika Najświętszego Serca Jezusowego Salezjanów). The presence of this huge building in what was previously a very poor district is somewhat surprising. Modelled on the basilica of San Paolo Fuori le Mura in Rome, the church was built just before World War I.

Further on, at Otwocka 14, is **Mała Warszawa** ⓭ (Little Warsaw), formerly Fabryka Trzciny, established by the composer Wojciech Trzciński. At various times, this complex of buildings has housed industry from plimsoll to tinned-meat factories. Today, it's a huge arts centre. All this is set within post-industrial interiors, where trolleys once used for carrying pigs' carcasses have been transformed into cloakroom hat stands, and thousands of bottles of methylated

spirit provide the backdrop for the buffet bars. Leaving the factory, go back to the tram terminus by the basilica, from where you can return to the city centre.

Food and drink

❶ **CENTRUM ZARZĄDZANIA ŚWIATEM**
Stefana Okrzei 26; tel: 022 618 2197; www.centrumswiata.com; Fri–Sat noon 3am, Sun Thu noon–midnight; €€
The juxtaposition of spacious industrial loft style within an historic tenement works very well at this restaurant/café/club and cultural centre. The stylish lamps are copies of those standing in the Praski Park, while the smoking area and toilets resemble sea containers. There is always something going on: concerts, stand-ups, workshops or poetry slams. Weekday menus are great value at 18zł. Try the local speciality, *tarte flambée* or *flammkuchen*, wafer-thin Alsatian bread with different toppings.

❷ **W OPARACH ABSURDU**
Ząbkowska 6; tel: 660 780 319; daily noon–2am; €
The eclectic interior is a blend of antique furniture market and a hippie commune from the 1970s. The short menu offers the classic Warsaw snacks to keep vodka company: herrings, tartar and pork jelly. Check out the *pierogi* happy hour: from Mon–Fri noon–4pm, the third portion is free. Good selection of beers and concerts in the evenings.

Strolling in Park Praski

NEW PRAGA

Despite its name, the borough comprises many historic buildings dating back to the turn of the 19th century. As the city's former industrial hub, New Praga still bears vestiges of that glorious past.

DISTANCE: 5.2km (3.2 miles)
TIME: 4 hours
START: Park Praski
END: Wileńska Metro Station
POINTS TO NOTE: Take bus 160 from the Central Railway Station or tram 23 or 26 from the Old Town to reach Park Praski. This tour can be easily combined with Route 12 (get a tram to the corner of Grochowska and Mińska). Although Stalowa street is much safer now than it used to be, it has retained some of its dubious reputation, so extra caution is advised.

When it comes to New Praga, the first thing that comes to mind are characterful alleys, fin-de siècle tenements with small dilapidated courtyards, and the notorious Stalowa street where the biggest steel mill in town once stood. These stereotypes arose as this once-prospering borough slowly fell into ruin. Fortuitously, what seemed to be an irreversible slide into oblivion was stopped and New Praga has had a new lease of life. Its famous alternative clubs on 11 Listopada street attract young people from across the river, while aspiring artists have moved in, lured by low rents and the creative atmosphere. The original residents may sometimes have a laugh or two about the strange mores of these newcomers, but once they settle in, they are embraced with open arms by the local community.

PARK PRASKI

Founded by the Tsar Aleksandr III, **Park Praski ❶** was opened to the public in 1871. Some of the trees in the park are 130 years old and include London planes, sweet chestnuts and Japanese gingkos as well as local species, such as poplars, lindens and maples. Next to the entrance of the park is one of Praga's most popular meeting points and a huge attraction for kids – an enclosure of brown bears, separated from Aleja Solidarności avenue by a ditch filled with water. It is been hotly debated whether a noisy and busy street is the right environment for animals, so

Brown bears at Warsaw ZOO

recently the ZOO director propoposed the idea that when the current residents of the enclosure die, they should be sub-stituted with bronze statues.

Having strolled through the park, you reach Ratuszowa street and the main gate to Warsaw ZOO, with a tourist infor-mation office next to it. You can either continue to the zoological gardens or (particularly in summer) take a short detour to the beach (see box) which lies west of the Zoo entrance.

ZOO

Opened in 1928, **Warsaw ZOO** ❷ (http://zoo.waw.pl; daily until dusk, May–Sep Mon–Fri 9am–6pm, Sat–Sun until 7pm, ticket office closes one hour earlier) was bombed by the Nazis in September 1939. The most danger-ous animals had to be killed, but some escaped while others ended up in the cooking pots of the starving Varsovians. The most valuable specimens were sent

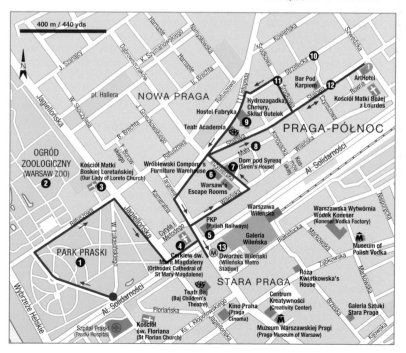

The lavish interior of the Cathedral of St Mary Magdalene

to Germany. During the German occupation, the ZOO director's Jan Żabiński and his wife Antonina saved countless Jewish orphans by hiding them in their villa, which still stands in the ZOO. After the war, they were both awarded with a honorary title of the 'Righteous Among the Nations'. Their story was told in the recent film *The Zookeeper's Wife*, starring Jessica Chastain as Antonina Żabińska. Among the highlights of the ZOO are the Hippopotamus House & Shark Aquarium, Ape House, Herpetarium and Aviary.

To the right of the ZOO gate (on the corner of Ratuszowa and Jagiellońska) stands **Our Lady of Loreto Church ③** (Kościół Matki Boskiej Loretańskiej).

The Vistula's beach

Boasting sunbeds, wicker chairs, volleyball and badminton courts, as well as a rope park and DJs sets at night, the beach on the Vistula's bank here is a popular place to unwind. It also offers unrivalled views of the Old Town across the river. Next to the beach is a ferry stop, where you can go to catch a boat across the river to the Fountain Park (see page 41) at the foot of New Town. It can take up to 40 people with bicycles and operates on weekends and holidays from April 29 to September 10 (in July–August also on weekdays, check the timetable at www.ztm.waw.pl). Best of all, it's totally free!

Built in 1640–44, it is the oldest in Praga. Designed by royal architect Constante Tencalla, its major attraction is a 15th century Gothic figure of Our Lady of Kamionek.

ORTHODOX CATHEDRAL OF ST MARY MAGDALENE

Continue on Jagiellońska and then turn right into Solidarności Avenue, heading towards Targowa. On your left you will soon see the onion-like domes of the **Orthodox Cathedral of St Mary Magdalene ④** (Cerkiew św. Marii Magdaleny), completed in 1869 as a symbol of the Russian domination. The church survived the war almost unscathed and its interior, including golden altars, has retained its original form. Worth noticing is the lavishly decorated Ikonostas. Outside the church stands an iron cross commemorating the carnage of Praga's residents by troops of the Russian general Suvorov in 1794. At the corner of Targowa and Solidarności Avenue, don't miss the monumental modernist **building of the Polish Railways ⑤** (PKP) designed by Marian Lalewicz in 1931. Keep walking along Targowa and then turn first into Wileńska street and then Inżynerska.

INŻYNIERSKA STREET

Just round the corner, at no.3, a big castle-like building made of red brick was originally the **Wróblewski company's**

View of the Old Town from the beach

furniture warehouse ❻, where Varsovians stored their furniture when they were emptying a rented flat or leaving for a long summer holiday. Now the building has been taken over by art galleries and artists' workshops. Among those who live and create here is sculpture, video and installation artist, Paweł Althamer. Opposite, at no.6, is the **Siren's House** ❼ (Dom pod Syreną). Decorated with the city's symbol the building once housed the oldest tram depot in town. It was from here that on 11 December 1866, the first horse-drawn tram hit the streets of Warsaw. Look out for the fragments of rails in the gates of the house. Follow Inżynierska and before turning right into **11 Listopada**, catch a glimpse of the picturesque **Mała street** ❽ lined on both sides with 19th-century buildings. A film-makers' favourite place to shoot period pieces, it was a perfect setting for Roman Polański's *The Pianist*, among others.

11 LISTOPADA STREET

With a cluster of atmospheric clubs including Hydrozagadka (www.hydrozagadka.waw.pl), Chmury (facebook.com/kawiarniachmury) and Skład Butelek (www.skladbutelek.pl), all located around a backyard at **no.22** ❾, this area of New Praga is definitely the place to be on a weekend night. Once the trendiest clubbing zone in Warsaw, it is much calmer now, but has retained its unique character. Besides clubs, there is also the **Hostel Fabryka** (www.hostelfabryka.pl) at no.22/21, located in a former rubber products' plant. Nearby, you can also find a theatre (Teatr Academia; www.teatracademia.com) and a photographic studio.

STRZELECKA AND ŚRODKOWA STREETS

At the T junction, first turn right and then immediately left into **Strzelecka street** ❿. At the corner of Środkowa stands a rather neglected building. It used to be home to the New Praga founder – Ksawery Konopacki, dating from 1864. At that time, the intersec-

Making the most of summer on the Vistula beach

'East Warsaw' by Sebas Velasco

tion of these two streets was a central point of the then-new settlement. At Strzelecka 26, don't miss an interesting mural called *East Warsaw* by world-famous street artist – Sebas Velasco. It was created during Street Art Doping festival. At no.17 on **Środkowa street** ⑪, you can see the *Warsaw Fight Club* mural, made by Conor Harrington during the same festival. At no.9, there is a unique, low wooden house (one of the few remaining in Warsaw) with a decorative façade. Dating from 1915, it housed a shelter for orphans and unattended children run by Kazimierz Lisiecki, known as 'Dziadek' (Grandfather), from 1934 to 1976.

Food and drink

① ARTBISTRO

Stalowa 52, tel: 022 252 05 03; http://artbistro.pl; daily 7am–10pm; €€€

Located in a beautifully converted old tenement, next to Aparthotel, this is a very atmospheric place with a modern, glass-enclosed patio, framed by bare brick walls. Traditional, familiar dishes made of fresh ingredients are presented in a modern way. The three-course lunch menu (21zł) is a budget option. Dishes ordered from the main menu may cost twice as much. There are also several breakfast menus to choose from (14zł). Early booking is recommended.

STALOWA STREET

From Środkowa turn into **Stalowa** ⑫, the largest and most important street in historic New Praga. Lined with acacias, it is pleasantly shady in summer. The street took its name (Steel street) after a steel mill that operated in the area in the 19th century. It boasted the most stylish tenements, the most attractive shops, plenty of workshops and a tram. After World War II the street's reputation was tarnished by blood-curdling accounts of vicious crimes, vengeance and cruelty. No wonder, for a long time it was a no-go zone for the 'foreigners' from the left bank of the river. Recently, Stalowa – just like the whole of Praga – has experienced architectural, social and cultural revival and now features numerous modern art galleries, antique shops and fashion boutiques. It has been used as a setting for numerous films including *Miasto 44*, *Time of Honour* (a popular TV series set in occupied and post-war Warsaw), *The Pianist* and many more. It's a pleasant place for a stroll with a few good refueling options, including Bar Pod Karpiem at no.37, with nicely-priced home-made lunch menus. The more elegant **ArtBistro**, see ①, at no.52 is located in a beautifully restored old tenement, also housing **Aparthotel**. From Stalowa retrace your steps to the corner of Targowa and Aleja Solidarności to get to the **Wileńska Metro Station** ⑬.

House and garden in Saska Kępa

SASKA KĘPA

This route takes in Saska Kępa, a favourite playground of the Saxon kings, featuring fine examples of Polish functionalism and some of the best eating options in town.

DISTANCE: 2.9km (1.8 miles)
TIME: Two hours
START/END: Waszyngton Roundabout
POINTS TO NOTE: Take tram 9 or 24 from Jerozolimskie Avenue to get to Waszyngton square. It is also possible to go by metro, but the station (Stadion Narodowy) is a long walk from the stadium. This route can be followed by Route 14.

Food and drink

① KUCHNIA FUNKCJONALNA

Jakubowska 16 (entrance from Estońska), tel: 512 893 898; daily 11am–11pm; €€
The domain of chef Bartosz Polak, who strives to make his dishes both tasty and beneficial to the body. Fresh, seasonal ingredients are carefully sourced and turned into a culinary pieces of art. On the menu you will find gluten-free and vegetarian options, but also a full English breakfast. Delicious home-made ice cream for dessert is a must.

Once an islet surrounded by the Vistula river, Saska Kępa did not receive its first inhabitants, five Dutch settlers fleeing religious persecution in their homeland, until the beginning of the 17th century. In 1735, King August III leased the whole area from the town for 30 years. It quickly became a favourite venue for parties and leisure activities, initially for the court and then for ordinary Warsaw residents, later in the 19th century. Saska Kępa ('Saxon Islet') was not connected with the left bank until the construction of the Poniatowski Bridge at the beginning of the 20th century. It was also when construction of elegant villas along the main thoroughfare, Francuska street, began.

FUNCTIONAL HOUSE

From the **Waszyngton Roundabout ①**, take Francuska, then turn right into Lipska street and right again into Estońska. At the end of the street, the **Functional House ②** (Dom Funcjonalny; Jakubowska 16; www.domfunkcjonalny. org) – designed in 1928 by the modernist architect Czesław Przybylski – is

Sculpture of Agnieszka Osiecka

on your left. Today it houses **BWA Gallery** (www.bwawarszawa.pl, Wed–Sat 2–6pm; free) and **Kuchnia Funkcjonalna ❶**. Head west on Jakubowska, turn left on Łotewska and into Berezyńska, which will lead to Francuska.

FRANCUSKA STREET

From here, head south down this elegant thoroughfare dotted with cafés and restaurants (mainly pizzerias and Asian eateries). Take a left into Walecznych street to reach **Przybytkowskich's House ❸** (Dom Przybytkowskich) at no.37. It is Saska Kępa's oldest and last wooden villa, dating from 1880. From here, follow Aldony street and turn right into Obrońców to get back to Francuska street. Across the street, next to the Rue de Paris café is a **monument to Agnieszka Osiecka ❹** (1936–1997). She was a famous poet, journalist and playwright, but most of all a prolific songwriter who lived nearby. Across the street from Rue de Paris is **Eureka library**, known for its two Maine Coon cats called Cezar and Czaka. Go down Francuska to the south; at no.2 stands a villa by Lucjan Korngold and Piotr Lubiński with a characteristic terrace at the back.

The building is one of the best examples of functionalism in Saska Kępa, inspired by Le Corbusier.

KATOWICKA STREET

Next, turn right onto Zwycięzców street and head towards the river. Turn right into Katowicka and follow the street until you reach the corner of Obrońców. The tower-like front of **Felicja Trębicka's villa** at no.25 is the best example of pure Art Deco style in Warsaw. From here, go back to the Waszyngton Roundabout. An interesting place here is the **Milano ❺** (Rondo Waszyngtona 2a; Mon–Fri 11am–7pm, Sat 11am–3pm), a modern art gallery that cooperates with many well-known contemporary Polish artists.

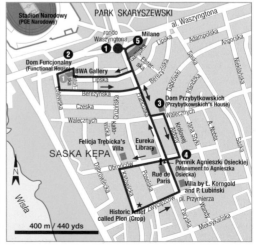

Stadion Narodowy's exterior

SKARYSZEWSKI PARK
AND MIŃSKA STREET

*This route wends through the Praga district from the ultramodern National
Stadium, a new symbol of the city, through the green oasis of Park Skaryszewski
to the beautifully converted post-industrial buildings of the Soho Factory.*

DISTANCE: 5.3km (3.3 miles)
TIME: Half a day with a lot of walking
START: National Stadium
END: Grochowska Street
POINTS TO NOTE: Take tram 9 or
24 from Aleje Jerozolimskie to get to
the National Stadium (stop Rondo
Waszyngtona). It is also possible to
go by metro, but the station (Stadion
Narodowy) is a long walk from the
stadium. This route can be followed
or preceded by Route 13 and Route
11 (tram 3, 6 or 26 from Grochowska
street to the Ząbkowska stop).

Quickly-changing Praga is now an artistic mecca where studios, galleries, alternative theatres and underground clubs mushroom, while modern housing estates rise on the abandoned post-industrial spaces. However, it also has a long history, longer in fact than most of the left bank settlements. In 1573, on the fields of the Kamion village, in the area adjacent to the present Skaryszewski Park, its residents witnessed the first free election of a Polish king. In the next centuries, the borough was destroyed several times (during the Swedish Deluge, the Kościuszko and November Uprisings) and each time painstakingly rebuilt. Before World War II it became the industrial hub of the capital, with many factories located in Kamion. Fortunately, South Praga was largely spared the ill fate of the left bank part of the city during World War II, so quite a few buildings dating to the turn of the 19th century survived.

NATIONAL STADIUM

TheNational Stadium, commonly known as **Stadion Narodowy** ❶ (PGE Narodowy; www.pgenarodowy.pl; guided tours daily), rises on the right bank of Vistula and has always been a symbolic place in the city's post war history. Built for the 2012 UEFA European Championships, it was constructed on top of its ruined predecessor – the 10th Anniversary Stadium, where the Polish national football team played some of its matches and the communist authorities organised annual harvest festivals and other propaganda

Poniatówka Beach

events. At the end of the 1980s, the stadium – by now in poor condition – was leased by the city authorities and turned into the biggest open-air market in this part of Europe, Jarmark Europa, which for the next decade attracted traders from every corner of the former Soviet Union and beyond, and played an important role in the city's economic growth.

The new stadium is a state-of-the art sport venue with a retractable roof,

58,000 seats and four huge LCD display screens. It hosts sport events, concerts and international conferences (the NATO summit was held here in 2016), while in winter, the central area of the pitch is occupied by an ice rink. The stadium's façade is made of a special mesh painted in silver and red, resembling Poland's national colours (white-red) from afar. It looks particularly impressive when lit up at night.

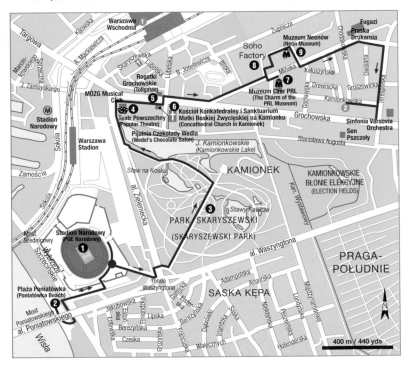

Inside Stadion Narodowy

Skaryszewski Park

Next to the stadium, on the riverbank, lies **Poniatówka Beach ❷** (Plaża Poniatówka), one of the main municipal beaches. A wood pavilion on the beach housing restrooms, toilets and showers cost 4 million zlotys (€1million) to build and has been called the most expensive urinal in town. Soon the beach will feature a sports area.

SKARYSZEWSKI PARK

Northeast of the roundabout lies the green expanse of the scenic **Skaryszewski Park ❸** (Park Skaryszewski), a fine example of Secessionist and early Modernist horticultural design, established between 1905 and 1922. Walking along its avenues, you pass clumps of ancient trees, ponds, and huge clearings adorned with excellent sculptures. Particularly impressive are three figures dating from the late 1920s: *Woman Bathing* by Olga Niewska, *Dancer* by Stanisław Jackowski, and *Rhythm* by Henryk Kuna. There is also a small monument, unveiled by Margaret Thatcher in 1988, commemorating the crew of a British bomber shot down over Warsaw by the Germans on 14 August 1944 and another one (next to the entrance) commemorating Polish victims of the terrorist attacks in New York. Head through the park to reach **Kamionkowskie Lake**, a remnant of the old Vistula river bed.

Next turn left into an alley leading to Zieleniecka Avenue. Continue north until you see the building of an old warehouse now housing the **Popular Theatre ❹** (Teatr Powszechny; www.powszechny. com) on the right. Besides the theatre, there is also a MÓZG musical club, the main jass centre (jass is a fusion of jazz, techno and folk) in Poland.

Passing the theatre, turn right into the wide Grochowska street. Nearby are two neoclassical **tollgates ❺** (Rogatki Grochowskie) from the early 19th century, through which visitors would pass when entering the city. The south one serves as Pijalnia Czekolady Wedla (Wedel's Chocolate Salon). Just beyond are the grey buildings of the **Wedel Chocolate Factory** (Fabryka Czekolady Emila Wedla), built in the inter-war period, although the company's history goes back to 1845. Further on is the **Concathedral Church in Kamionek ❻** (Kościół Konkatedralny i Sanktuarium Matki Boskiej Zwycięskiej na Kamionku); a bit uninspiring, but the cemetery is one of the oldest historic sites in Warsaw, and a kind of military pantheon, with the gravestones of soldiers from numerous countries. Leaving the church behind, cross the Grochowska street and turn left into Mińska street.

MIŃSKA

A typical Warsaw mix of old and new buildings, Mińska has several attractions to offer. Walk until you see a small Fiat signposting the entrance to **The Charm of the PRL Museum ❼** (Muzeum Czar PRL; Mińska 25, entrance from Głucha street; http://czarprl.pl; Mon–Fri 10am–4pm,

Nysa vans displayed in front of The Charm of the PRL Museum

Sat–Sun 11am–7pm). Located in a former Polish Optical Factory (PZO) which hasn't changed a bit since the 1950s, it is a private collection of everyday items (radios, photographic cameras, tennis racquets, bicycles, TV sets and more) from the bygone era when the country's official name was the People's Republic of Poland (PRL in Polish). You can hire an English-speaking guide who will walk you through the exhibition.

SOHO FACTORY

Having seen the museum, cross Mińska and follow through the gate to **Soho Factory** ❽ – a revitalised industrial area covering more than 8 hectares (19.7 acres). The red brick building right to the gate was part of the first ammunition plant opened in 1925. After World War II, the factory was rebuilt and churned out motorcycles

Recreated living room at the PRL museum

as well as the Polish version of the Vespa scooter, called Osa (Wasp). The revitalisation of this industrial area was modelled after the regeneration of New York's Meatpacking District. Ultramodern housing blocks stand next to the converted industrial buildings, now housing everything from a coffee roaster to two theatres, a tattoo salon and a museum. Soho Factory is also a popular venue of cultural events and exhibitions. **Warszawa Wschodnia**, see ❶, owned by Mateusz Gessler, is the perfect place to stop.

Neon Museum

One of the major attractions of Soho Factory is the excellent **Neon Museum** ❾ (Muzeum Neonów; www.neonmuzeum. org; Mińska 25, building 55; Wed–Fri noon–5pm, Sat 11am–6pm, Sun 10am–5pm) housing an interesting collection of Cold War-era neon signs and other electro-graphic artefacts. Most of them were designed by top graphic designers who were also behind the so called Polish Poster School. The exhaustive information panels provide much needed cultural and political background.

ALONG MIŃSKA

Continue along Mińska to the former October Revolution Printing House (Drukarnia im. Rewolucji Październikowej) at no.65, now a multipurpose cultural and educational complex with artists and designers' workshops and practice rooms. It also houses two clubs: Praska

The Neon Museum

Drukarnia and the reactivated Fugazi, with a bar in the shape of a guitar. From here, take Terespolska street back to Grochowska. From Terespolska you can take a short detour to **Pasta**, see ❷, at Kamionkowska 48a, boasting a pleasant summer garden.

GROCHOWSKA

Just around the corner on Grochowska street stands the building of the **Sinfonia Varsovia Orchestra** (Sinfonia Varsovia Orchestra, www.sinfoniavarsovia.org), which along with the adjacent area will be soon converted into a state-of-the-art musical centre, including a new 1,800-seat concert hall, restaurants, cafés and a French garden.

Cross Grochowska and head north, passing a row of townhouses. After less than 200 metres (656ft), you come to **Perun** factory (www.perun.pl) at no 301/305, on the left, the only one in town to continue manufacturing the same product (welding equipment) for more than a century. Part of the plant is now occupied by a climbing wall and a cultural centre **Bee's Dream** (Sen Pszczoły; www.senpszczoly.pl) also a popular concert venue. Behind the factory lies a wide stretch of green adjacent to Skaryszewski Park. This is Election Fields (Błonia Elekcyjne), where Polish noblemen first gathered to freely elect their king in 1573.

You can end the tour on Grochowska street or catch a tram and after a few stops, continue on Route 11.

Food and drink

❶ WARSZAWA WSCHODNIA

Mińska 25, tel: 022 870 2918; www.mateuszgessler.com.pl; daily 24 hrs; €€€–€€€€

Owned by Mateusz Gessler, self-proclaimed aficionado of good food, Warszawa Wschodnia offers a combination of traditional Polish dishes with a dash of nouvelle cuisine française. Mains include a flagship Beef Wellington, rabbit in mustard sauce and deer medallions, while there are also fish and veggie options. The central point of the sleek modern interior is a huge open kitchen, allowing customers to watch as their meals are being prepared. There is also a less formal summer garden outside. Quite amazingly, the restaurant is open around the clock. Set lunch menus are a real bargain (25zł) at this otherwise expensive establishment.

❷ RESTAURACJA PASTA

Kamionkowska 48a; tel: 022 464 8241; www.restauracjapasta.pl; Tue–Sun noon–8pm; €€

A short menu based on fresh, seasonal ingredients including staples such as pierogi and *placki ziemniaczane* (potato pancakes) as well as soups and pastas, plus a modest selection of entries such as beef and salmon tartar served with homemade bread. The main asset is, however, a lovely summer garden with a 70-year old walnut tree and two fountains.

DIRECTORY

Hand-picked hotels and restaurants to suit all budgets and tastes, organised by area, plus select nightlife listings, an alphabetical listing of practical information, a language guide and an overview of the best books and films to give you a flavour of the city.

The Bristol

ACCOMMODATION

Warsaw is home to a growing number of modern hotels belonging to large international chains, mainly in the city centre. By the end of 2017, two more luxury establishments will open in the capital; the five star Renaissance Hotel (part of the Marriott chain), with proximity to the airport, and the historic Europejski Hotel, once it is open in 2017, expected to be the most luxurious in the entire country. Budget travellers may have less options to choose from, but nevertheless, the hotels in this bracket have dramatically changed for the better over the last few years. The number of hostels (mainly private) has substantially increased, while ever since Euro 2012, more and more apartments are also being let to tourists through small firms, as well as private individuals (it's not always legal though). For apartments to let, check out the following websites: www.pandoapartments.com.pl and www.apartmentsambasada.com. As usual, accommodation prices vary by season, but still compare favourably with most Western capitals. Booking well ahead can go a long way in finding rates at three or four-star hotels that are only slightly higher than those in hostels. According to Europe Backpacker Index 2017, Warsaw rates among the top ten budget-friendly city destinations in Europe.

Old Town

Castle Inn
Świętojańska 2; tel. 022 425 01 00; http://castleinn.pl; €€€
The biggest asset of this small, quirky hotel (just 22 rooms) is its location in the Old Town, only a few steps from the Castle Square. Each room (they are very small!) has different décor, inspired by works of Rene Magritte or Lewis Carroll. Some have views over the Castle. It's an ideal place for lovers of a romantic ambience.

Old Town Kanonia Hostel & Apartments
Jezuicka 2; tel: 022 635 06 76; www.kanonia.pl; €
One of the oldest hostels in Warsaw and the only one located in the Old Town. The great views over the Kanonia Square and Dawna Street compensate a little bit for the less sophisticated interiors. Also offers private apartments scattered around the Old Town.

> The price categories below reflect the average rate for a double room in high season without breakfast:
> €€€€ = over 600zł
> €€€ = 300–600zł
> €€ = 150–300zł
> € = below 150zł

A luxurious room at the Bristol

Around Krakowskie Przedmieście

Bellotto

Senatorska 13/15; tel: 022 829 64 44; www.hotelbellotto.pl; €€€€
Located in the former Primate's Palace, dating back to the 16th century, this 5-star hotel is very close to the Old Town and the Royal Route. Focaccia Ristorante offers delicious Italian dishes with a modern twist. Breakfast buffet from 7.30am.

Bristol

Krakowskie Przedmieście 42/44; tel: 022 551 1000; www.hotelbristolwarsaw.pl; €€€€
Warsaw's most prestigious hotel boasts a superb location right in the middle of the Royal Route, next to the Presidential Palace. Combining a neo-Renaissance façade with luxury interiors, this historic hotel was founded by Ignacy Paderewski – a Polish piano virtuoso and internationally acclaimed composer, as well as statesman. Bristol opened its doors in 1901 and since then has hosted a plethora of world celebrities including the likes of Pablo Picasso, Marlene Dietrich, Sophia Loren, Woody Allen and Martin Scorsese.

Dream Hostel Warszawa

Krakowskie Przedmieście 55, tel: 022 419 48 49; http://dream-hostels.com; €
This joyfully decorated and clean hostel is located right on Krakowskie Przed-mieście (Royal Route). The curtains on every bunk-bed are a great idea, providing a little bit of much welcome privacy. Private rooms are also available.

Harenda

Krakowskie Przedmieście 4–6; tel: 022 826 0071; www.hotelharenda.com.pl; €€€
This is in a great location near the university on one of Warsaw's finest streets, a few minutes' walk from the Old Town. Rooms are modern and plainly furnished. There's a lively club (of the same name) next door.

Around Nowy Świat

Mamaison Hotel Le Regina Warsaw

Chmielna 13A; tel: 022 505 91 00; www.mamaisondiana.com; €€€
The location just off the Chmielna Street separates it from street noise, but still gives easy access to good shopping areas, nightlife and Royal Route (Nowy Świat). It offers 46 studios and apartments with kitchenettes. A good option for a longer stay.

Patchwork Design Hostel

Chmielna 5/7; tel: 022 258 39 59; www.patchworkhostel.pl; €
Located at one of the courtyards off Chmielna street, this hostel offers easy access to the capital's nightlife zones. It has 6, 8 and 10 bed dormitories as well as twins and doubles with shared bathrooms. Simple white interiors are livened with splashes of colour.

Residence St Andrew's Palace

Chmielna 30; tel: 22 826 46 40;
http://residencestandrews.pl; €€€

24 apartments occupy a beautifully restored old townhouse on one of the most popular pedestrianised shopping streets in the city. All the apartments – for two, three or four persons – have a bathroom, kitchen and living room. Single travellers can opt for a studio flat with sofa-bed and open kitchen.

SixtySix Hotel

Nowy Świat 66; tel: 022 826 61 11;
www.hotelsixtysix.com; €€€€

This modern and elegant boutique hotel occupies an old townhouse at the Royal Route. The 18 rooms ooze sophistication and have all the amenities a demanding guest would expect. Best of all, the hotel is environment-friendly.

Around Łazienki

Agrykola

Myśliwiecka 9; tel: 022 622 9110;
www.agrykola-noclegi.pl; €

This good value hostel near Łazienki Park and Ujazdowski Castle is aimed primarily at student sports groups and offers simple accommodation about 3km (1.8 miles) from the city centre as well as a great view of the castle. Breakfast available at extra cost.

Regent Hotel Warsaw

Belwederska 23; tel: 22 558 1234;
www.regent-warsaw.com; €€€€

The luxury Regent Warsaw Hotel is superbly located next to Łazienki Park at the corner of Belwederska and Spacerowa streets. 246 rooms include luxury suites, while the hotel restaurant, Venti-tre, serves excellent Italian cuisine. The hotel also includes a spa, plus a gym and aerobics studio. The famous people who have slept here include former Russian President Dmitry Medvedev and the Rolling Stones. It was also the headquarters of the Polish national football team during Euro 2012.

Powiśle

Ibis Budget Warszawa Centrum

Zagórna 1; tel: 022 7453660;
www.ibis.com; €

Yet another budget option, the 176 rooms here are basic, clean and have private bathrooms. The main asset is the location, by the riverside in the very popular Powiśle borough. It's a good starting point to explore the Górnośląska and Rozbrat streets, which are lined with restaurants, and the nice park close by.

City Centre

Campanile

Towarowa 2; tel: 022 582 7200;
www.campanile.com.pl; €€

Inside the same huge building as two other hotels, the city-centre air-conditioned Campanile is benefitting from an upgrade taking place throughout the

chain. It may be characterless, but for its value, service and facilities it really is hard to beat.

H15

Poznańska 15; tel: 022 553 87 77; www.h15boutiqueapartments.com; €€€€

This five-star hotel is housed in a 19th century building, thoroughly renovated to the highest standard. 46 elegant apartments stand out thanks to their modern design and comfort. The beautiful courtyard is covered with a glass roof, creating a good place for breakfast.

Hampton by Hilton

Wspólna 72; tel: tel: 022 317 2700; www.hiltonhotels.com; €€

Only a short walk from the Central Railway Station, the Palace of Culture and the lively Koszyki market, this modern hotel features 300 rooms, business and fitness centres, free internet and breakfast included in the price of room.

Hostel Centrum Warszawa

Emili Plater 36A; tel: 022 652 00 10; http://warsawhostelcentrum.pl; €

Located near lively Grzybowski Square, this hostel offers the possibility of learning more about Poland. It is decorated with wallpaper presenting old photos of Warsaw and famous Polish people. The knowledgeable staff is a big asset. It only has dormitories, but is well-equipped with private lamps and lockers.

Intercontinental

Ul. Emilii Plater 49; tel: 022 328 88 88; www.warszawa.intercontinental.com; €€€

This modern, centrally located hotel is one of the tallest buildings in the city. Conveniently located, it is just a stone's throw from most tourist attractions including the Palace of Culture, the Warsaw Uprising Museum and the Old Town (a little bit farther). Offering breathtaking views over the city, it has 414 elegant rooms and an award-winning restaurant, Platter, by Karol Okrasa, one of the best known celebrity chefs in Poland, as well as a River-View Wellness Centre and Spa on the 43rd floor.

Maria Hotel

Al. Jana Pawła II 71; tel: 022 838 4062; www.hotelmaria.pl; €€€

A delightful family-run hotel near the Powązki and Jewish cemeteries and within walking distance of the Old Town. With friendly service and nicely furnished modern rooms, this is an especially good option for those who don't like big corporate hotels. The restaurant offers a nice variety of Polish and European dishes and a well-composed wine list. 24 rooms.

Marriott Warsaw

Al. Jerozolimskie 65–79; tel: 022 630 6306; www.marriott.com; €€€–€€€€

Luxurious modern high-rise in the city centre, with 10 restaurants, health club, swimming pool and penthouse cocktail bar.

MDM Hotel

Pl. Konstytucji 1; tel: 022 339 1600; www.hotelmdm.com.pl; €€

Large hotel centrally located on Constitution Square. The building is typical of 1950s Polish architecture, and the standard décor is rather anonymous, but rooms are large and it's a fair deal for the location.

Mercure Warsaw Grand

Krucza 28; tel: 022 5832100; www.mercure.com; €€

This four-star hotel is conveniently located in the city centre, just a few steps from Trzech Krzyży square and fashionable Mokotowska street. The building, now nicely renovated and equipped with all the amenities, was built in 1954–57 as part of the governmental quarter, so was designed in a typically socialist realist style.

Polonia Palace Hotel

Al. Jerozolimskie 45; tel: 022 318 2800; www.polonia palace.com; €€€

One of Warsaw's oldest hotels, immaculately restored with a Belle Époque restaurant and modern facilities, boasts a superb central location. Opened in 1913, it was the only hotel in town that survived the war, which is why it hosted many foreign embassies in the late 1940s. Strauss restaurant offers dishes that are a blend of Western and Eastern influences.

Rialto

Wilcza 73; tel: 022 584 87 00; www.rialto.pl; €€€€

This lovely boutique hotel is located in a superbly renovated Art Deco townhouse, only a few blocks from Koszyki market and numerous restaurants on Nowogrodzka and Poznańska streets. Each room is furnished with authentic Art Deco furniture, featuring high-quality materials including wood, stone cladding, glass mosaic and nickel-plated brass. Its top-class restaurant Salto is a domain of the Argentian chef Martín Gimenez Castro, winner of the first Polish edition of the TV show *Top Chef* and one of Warsaw's culinary celebrities. It boasts an excellent choice of fish and seafood options as well as great Argentinian steaks.

Sheraton Warsaw

Prusa 2; tel: 022 450 6100; www.sheraton.com.pl; €€€€

The hotel of choice for international business travellers, the very modern and elegant Sheraton is located halfway between Łazienki Park and the Old Town. Rooms are luxuriously appointed, and 'executive rooms' are completely outfitted with work facilities. Excellent gym, restaurants and services.

The Westin's striking glass lift

Warsaw Downtown Hostel

Wilcza 33; tel: 022 629 35 76;
www.warsawdowntown.pl; €

This has a great location, in an old house in the city centre. There are dormitories and private rooms, all with bathrooms. Guests can use the fully equipped kitchen and participate in the variety of special events organised almost every day, such as games, cooking, karaoke and film nights. Free breakfast.

Westin

Al. Jana Pawła 21; tel: 022 450 80 00;
www.westin.pl; €€€

One of many smart, modern hotels that has opened in Warsaw in the last few years, the Westin features an impressive external glass lift offering amazing views as you go up. Stylish, comfortable rooms have impressive bathrooms and some also have a view over the Palace of Culture. Families will be delighted with the kids' corner and childcare service (on demand). It lies very close to the Central Railway Station and Złote Tarasy commercial centre.

Praga

Aparthotel Stalowa52

Stalowa 52; tel: 022 618 27 32;
www.stalowa52.pl; €€

Located on one of the most charming streets in New Praga, this elegant hotel in an old renovated tenement house offers 19 rooms and two apartments in the city centre (Mokotowska and Ludna Street). It has a good restaurant next door, Art Bistro.

Near Fryderyk Chopin Airport

Holiday Inn Express Warsaw Airport

Poleczki 31; tel: 022 373 37 00;
www.ihg.com; €€

This is a good choice for those who need to stay near the airport (although in Warsaw the airport is just 8km (5 miles) away from the city centre). The hotel offers simply decorated rooms, clean bathrooms and a comfortable bed – all you need for a short stay. Surprisingly, despite the proximity to the airport and highway vicinity, the rooms are quiet.

WOK Camping

ul. Odrębna 16; tel: 022 612 79 51;
www.campingwok.warszawa.pl; €

Set in a quiet forest on the city's right riverbank, this campsite is only about 10km (6.2 miles) away from the city centre. Facilities include clean modern toilets, a barbecue garden, children's playground and launderette. There is also free Wi-Fi. Best of all, it also has a motel section, hence the camping is open all year round. A bus stop is less than 0.5km (0.3 miles) away. According to the Polish Federation of Camping and Caravanning, this is the best campsite in Warsaw and one of the best in Poland.

Marconi fine dining

RESTAURANTS

Old and New Town

Podwale 25 Piwna Kompania

ul. Podwale 25; tel: 022 635 63 14; www.podwale25.pl; Mon–Sat 11am–1am; Sun noon–midnight; €€

Traditional Polish cuisine is served in this convivial restaurant with a large courtyard for al fresco dining, set in the heart of the Old Town. It's famous for its pork knuckle, Schnitzel, *pierogi*, Polish gherkins, beer and soda water dispensed from a siphon seltzer bottle.

Przy Zamku

Pl. Zamkowy 15/19; tel: 0 660 155 164; daily 10am–11pm; €€€

The location and rather high prices may suggest a tourist trap, but the quality of food is outstanding. The décor of a stylish hunting lodge with stuffed animal heads on the walls may not be to everyone's liking, but it goes with traditional Polish *bigos* and game meat on the menu.

Around Krakowskie Przedmieście and Nowy Świat

Marconi

ul. Krakowskie Przedmieście 42–44; tel: 022 551 1832; www.restauracjamarconi.pl; daily 7am–10.30pm; €€€€

As you might expect from the Bristol Hotel, this is a refined, traditional restaurant serving excellent Polish and Italian cuisine. One of the city's most luxurious, sophisticated dining rooms.

Mąka i Woda

ul. Chmielna 13A; tel: 022 505 91 87; Mon–Fri noon–3pm, 4–10pm, Sat noon–11pm, Sun noon–8pm; €€

This modern and spacious restaurant in one of the courtyards off Chmielna Street is the perfect place to take a break from the city noise. It claims to serve the best Italian-style pizza in Warsaw. Besides classic and white pizzas, the menu includes salads, pasta and antipasti.

Senses

ul. Bielańska 12; tel: 022 331 96 97; http://sensesrestaurant.pl; Mon–Sat 6–21.45pm (last orders); €€€€

The second Polish restaurant to be awarded a Michelin star is the domain of Italian chef, Andrea Camastra. The seasonal tasting menu of 6 or 9 courses may include Polish and international dishes such as seafood goulash with octopus or *pierogi* with red prawns and smoked cream. It's a real treat for your senses.

Around Łazienki

Atelier Amaro €€€€

Ul. Agrykola 1; tel. 022 628 57 47; www.atelier amaro.pl; Mon–Sat lunch and dinner; €€€€.

The winner of the first Michelin star in Poland, Chef Modest Amaro creates innovative Polish cuisine using the freshest seasonal ingredients and sometimes featuring long-forgotten traditional products. The modern interior is

Steak and chips at Restauracja Polska Różana

cosy but small. Professional yet friendly service contributes to the relaxed atmosphere. Booking essential.

Restauracja Polska Różana
ul. Chocimska 7; tel: 022 848 12 25; www.restauracjarozana.com.pl; daily noon–last customer; €€€€

This is a beautifully decorated townhouse restaurant set in a romantic garden with splashing fountains, situated just off Plac Unii Lubelskiej. It boasts a wonderful selection of Polish dishes and vodkas to keep them company, followed by great meringue cakes and homemade cheesecake. The lunch menu (Mon–Fri) for 42zł is a good option.

Jewish Warsaw
Czerwony Wieprz
ul. Żelazna 68; tel: 022 850 31 44; www.czerwonywieprz.pl; daily for lunch and dinner; €€€

A themed restaurant (Czerwony Wieprz means Red Hog), this spot tries to recreate the atmosphere of communist Poland. Besides the extravagant decor and names of the dishes, it offers a really good example of the traditional Polish cooking that was popular 50 years ago.

> Price guide for a two-course meal for one without drinks:
> €€€€ = over 70zł
> €€€ = under 70zł
> €€ = under 50zł
> € = under 30zł

The menu includes beef tartare, pig trotters in aspic and Warsaw-style tripe soup. Round the corner at Waliców 13 is another branch, Folk Gospoda, specialising in Polish traditional cuisine.

Kieliszki na Próżnej
ul. Próżna 12; tel: 0 501 764 674; www.kieliszkinaproznej.pl; Mon–Wed noon–10pm, Thu–Sat noon–11pm; €€€€

As the name ('wine glasses at Próżna') and the impressive wine list may suggest, the wine – especially Italian bottles – plays a central role. Polish dishes with a modern twist are made from the freshest local products. Weekday lunch menus are only 35zł.

Thaisty
Pl. Bankowy 4, tel: 0 730 000 024 http://thaisty.pl; Mon 4–11pm, Tue–Sun 11am–11pm; €€€

This always-crowded restaurant serves arguably the best Thai food in Warsaw. In addition to the general menu with staples such as tom yum soup, pad Thai and green and red curry, chef Chanunkan Duangkumma prepares also special seasonal dishes. In summer the outdoor tables are a good place to sip cold Thai tea and watch people pass by.

Vege Miasto
ul. Solidarności 60a; tel: 022 252 0525; www.vegemiasto.pl; daily noon–9pm; €

Located in an old communist pavilion, this is a vegans' paradise. Pastas, hummus, pancakes, dumplings, soups, salads,

Duck with cranberry at Dyspensa

delicious colourful cakes and desserts all made with vegan ingredients make it hard to choose. To ease your selection, there are set lunch menus available for just 25zł. Some tables are placed right in the windows. Excellent choice of teas, coffees and juices/smoothies.

City Centre

Bar Mleczny Prasowy (Prasowy Milk Bar)

ul. Marszałkowska 10/16; tel: 666 353 776; http://prasowy.pl/; Mon–Fri 9am–8pm, Sat–Sun 11am–7pm; €

This is a modern incarnation of the old Bar Mleczny Prasowy. Milk bars were common in communist Poland, providing the working classes with cheap and (supposedly) healthy food. The first thing you see is a long queue, not surprising in a place where you can eat a bowl of soup for 2zł or *pierogi* for 6zł. It's not just a bar, there are a lot of cultural events going on.

Bibenda

ul. Nowogrodzka 10; tel: 502 77 03 03; http://bibenda.pl; Tue–Sun noon–10pm; €€

A trendy place on Nowogrodzka, the short menu here includes dishes made from fresh, locally sourced ingredients. Fish and vegetarian options abound (try cod with barley or mushroom risotto). It can get very crowded at night.

Butchery & Wine

ul. Żurawia 22; tel: 022 502 31 18; www.butcheryandwine.pl; Mon–Sat noon–10pm, Sun until 8pm; €€€€

This airy, simple and understatedly smart restaurant is a paradise for meat lovers and serves arguably the best steaks in Warsaw. Wines are carefully selected; you can even sample a Polish one from the Lubuskie region. Prices are high, but you won't regret it.

Charlotte

Pl. Zbawiciela; tel: 662 20 45 55; http://bistrocharlotte.pl; open Mon-Thu 7am–midnight, Fri 7am–1am, Sat 9am–1am, Sun 9am–10pm (till midnight in summer); €€

This hugely popular bistro at the hipster Plac Zbawiciela is famous for its home-made bread, which forms the base for their French inspired menu.

Dyspensa

ul. Mokotowska 39; tel: 022 629 99 89, www.dyspensa.pl; open daily noon–last customer; €€€€

A terrific-looking place decked out to look like a welcoming country kitchen. Very popular and atmospheric at night, when locals and ex-pats pack in to enjoy international and Polish dishes, including duck with cranberry and zander with crayfish.

Krowarzywa

ul. Marszałkowska 27/35; tel: 0 516 894 767; http://krowarzywa.pl; daily noon–11pm; €

The tasty vegan burgers served here are made only from natural and seasonal products and are popular with even non-vegetarians. The secret ingredients are superfoods like spirulina, goji berries and barley grass powder.

Cosy and traditonal Stary Dom

La Sirena

Piękna 54; tel: 690 08 50 54; Mon–Thu noon–11pm, Fri–Sat until 2am, until 11pm on Sun; €€

The second venture by the owners of the famous Dziurka od klucza (see page 70) restaurant in Powiśle is a dodgy-looking mini-bar modelled after Mexican drinking dens. The interior is cramped and simple with bare walls and Mexican-styled ornaments. However, they do excellent – if not cheap – cocktails and a selection of staple Mexican dishes.

Prodiż Warszawski

ul. Poznańska 16; tel: 022 127 71 71; http://prodizwarszawski.pl; Sun–Wed noon–11pm, Thu–Sat noon–1am; €€€

This little restaurant in the basement of a townhouse has an old-fashioned ambience underlined by brick walls and the popular 1970s songs played. It serves crayfish soup, Baltic herring, veal-stuffed *pierogi* and other traditional Polish staples. Good Polish beers and amazing meringue cake are definitely worth a try.

Shipudei Berek

ul. Jasna 20; tel: 022 826 25 10; http://berekwarszawa.pl; Mon–Sat 8am–midnight, Sun from 10am; €€

In this modern, colourful grill bar, Israeli chef Ofir Vidavsky serves staples of the Mediterranean and Eastern kitchen such as mezze, vegetarian and meat skewers, hummus and authentic shakshuka for breakfast. Lunch and breakfast fixed menus are really good value.

Mokotów

Mezze

ul. Różana 1; tel: 662 987 617; daily 11am–10pm; €

Definitely one of the best falafel and hummus spots in town, this popular vegetarian restaurant offers Middle Eastern staples including shakshuka and a great variety of hummus, as well as roasted eggplant. The servings are generous and prices very reasonable. A good place for quick lunch.

Stary Dom

ul. Puławska 104/106; tel: 022 646 42 08; www.restauracjastarydom.pl; daily noon–11.30pm; €€€

The old-fashioned décor makes you feel that you're in a smart and cosy mountain chalet. The menu includes the biggest staples of traditional Polish cuisine: platters of charcuterie and pâtés, Kashubian-style herring, pork knuckle, goose, ducks and *pierogi*. Watch out for big portions. Booking essential.

Tbilisi

Puławska 24; tel: 739 631 296; www.tbilisi.waw.pl; daily noon-10pm

Home-made Georgian cuisine at its best. This cosy, rustic place in Mokotów offers a variety of *kchachapuri* (traditional bread filled with cheese) as well as a selection of delicious meat and vegetarian dishes. Famous Georgian wines and Borjomi mineral water should not be missed either. Booking advisable as the restaurant is rather small.

Old Town bars filling up

NIGHTLIFE

Warsaw is deservedly famous for its diverse and lively night scene. The wealthy keep to glamorous clubs in the centre of town (Teatralny and Piłsudskiego squares, Mazowiecka street) while young and alternative crowds choose the riverbank or quirky spots in Praga, around Plac Zbawiciela or in up-and-coming Saska Kępa. No matter what your taste and how deep your pockets, the city will gladly satisfy everyone from glitz-lovers to hardcore ravers. Clubs and bars go in and out of fashion so quickly that the best thing is to ask a local for advice.

Beer and vodka bars

With the craft beer revolution in full swing, beer bars have become one of Warsaw's specialities. There are now dozens of places offering a mind-blowing variety of beers (on tap and bottled) on every corner, at least in the centre. The most popular ones include **Cuda na Kiju** (in the former communist party headquarters next to de Gaulle's roundabout), **Kufle i Kapsle** (Nowogrodzka 25), **Piw Paw** (Foksal 16) or **Same Krafty** (Nowomiejska 10). Beer bars also serve another recent Polish craft speciality – cider. Equally popular, particularly among tourists, are bars serving shots of vodka and traditional snacks (including herring, beef tartar and pork jelly). Among the most fashionable are **Pijalnia Wódki i Piwa** (Nowy Świat 19a) and **Bar & Res-** taurant **Warszawa** (Krakowskie Przedmieście 79), which also offers live music Thu–Fri from 8.30pm, with DJs taking over the floor from midnight Fri–Sat.

Riverbank bars

When it is warm enough (usually from early May), the party moves to the numerous venues on the left riverbank, with a string of clubs, bars and eateries stretching from Łazienkowski Bridge to Gdański Bridge. Beloved of local hipsters, **Plac Zabaw** (Bulwar Grzymały Siedleckiego) is not only a bar with live music at night, but also a cultural centre, presenting film screenings, comedy performances, workshops for children, and slow market bazaars. Its younger sibling **BarKa** (near Copernicus Science Centre) is famous for alternative music concerts.

There are literally dozens of beach bars and night clubs by the river each year, with most of them emerging and equally swiftly disappearing. The best way to enjoy them is to simply walk along the Vistula boulevards, stopping when you like.

Bars

BarStudio
Pl. Defilad 1 (Palace of Culture); tel: 603 300 835; daily 9am–1am; www.barstudio.pl
This hip bar in the Palace of Culture with nice outside tables in summer is more of a drinking den than dance club and is famous for its Sunday buffet breakfast.

Alfresco drinks on the terrace of a Vistula beach disco

Panorama Sky Bar

Aleje Jerozolimskie 65/79; tel: 022 630 74 35;
http://panoramaskybar.pl; daily 6pm–2am

Arguably the coolest bar with a view in
town is located on the 40th floor of the
Marriott hotel. The views are spectacular and so are the pricey cocktails served
in a modern and luxurious interior.

Plan B

Al. Wyzwolenia 18; tel: 503 116 154; daily
11am–2am, until midnight on Sun

Located at the heart of the fun zone at
Zbawiciela Square, this spot has spar-
tan décor, but it's always full and the rev-
elry often spills into the street. Excellent
music, drinks at reasonable prices and
an international environment.

Warszawa Powiśle

Kruczkowskiego 3B; tel: 022 474 40 84;
daily 9am–midnight (until 2am Fri–Sat)

With plenty of deckchairs set around
a concrete rotunda, this is a favourite
meeting place for crowds heading to or
from parties on the riverbank. Beers and
cocktails galore plus good music make
this the perfect watering hole.

Live music

Hydrozagadka

11 Listopada 22; tel: 0502 070 916;
www.hydrozagadka.waw.pl

This legendary club in Praga is a typical
underground venue: a bit rough, not very
clean, uncompromising in design and
attracting people from all walks of life.
Alternative music gigs are a major draw.

Klub Hybrydy

Złota 7/9, tel: 022 822 8702;
http://hybrydy.com.pl

A legendary club that has been around
since the late 1950s. Today it attracts
mainly students, with disco nights taking
place Thu–Sat from 8pm. It also hosts
concerts, comedy shows and exhibitions.

Stodoła

Batorego 10; tel: 022 825 60 31;
www.stodola.pl

Opened in 1956, this legendary student
club used to be a shrine for Warsaw's
jazz bands; it also played a major role in
the Polish rock explosion in the 1980s.
Now it hosts concerts by the best Polish
and major international artists.

Nightclubs

Enklawa

Mazowiecka 12; tel: 022 827 31 51;
www.enklawa.com; Tue–Sat 10pm–4am

One of the best clubs, this is known
for keeping up with the latest clubbing
trends. Live music and fashion events
attract a posh crowd. Wednesday's Old
School Night (mainly 1970's and 80's
sounds) enjoys a legendary status.

XOXO

Marii Konopnickiej 6; tel: 665 22 52 26;
www.xoxoishere.com; Fri–Sat 10pm–5am

A huge dance floor, numerous bars, private and VIP areas make XOXO a perfect place for events including fashion
shows. In order to stand a chance of getting in, you need to dress to impress.

Eateries line the Old Town Market Place

A–Z

A

Admission charges

Most museums charge between 15 and 30zł for entry, with reductions for children, students and families.

Age restrictions

The age of consent in Poland is 15. You must be 18 to buy alcohol and could be asked to present ID if you look particularly young. There is no minimum legal age for drinking alcohol. The minimum age for car hire is usually 21; some companies charge an extra fee for drivers younger than 30.

B

Budgeting

Accommodation: Visitors to Warsaw are now spoilt for choice as far as accommodation is concerned. From large international chains such as Marriott, Sheraton or Hyatt to small boutique hotels located in a beautifully restored historical buildings, Warsaw has much to offer even to the most demanding clientele. The possibilities at the lower end are also expanding every day with hostels and cheap apartments springing up across the city. An average price (high season) for a double room in a budget hotel/apartment in the city cen-

tre will cost from 200zł (€50), a mid-range hotel will set you back around 400zł (€100) while night at one of the best hotels might cost around 900zł (€210). You will be charged around 40zł (€10) for a bed in a common dormitory at a youth hostel.

Eating out: A main course at a restaurant: budget 15–30zł (€3.50–4.70), mid-range 40–50zł (€7–10) and expensive upwards of 60zł (€12–14). A glass of wine will set you back 12–15zł (€2.80–3.52), a pint of local draught beer 8–10zł (€1.90–2.30) while a cup of coffee (espresso) can be had from 8zł (€2).

Single bus/tram/metro ticket: A 4.40zł (€1.03) ticket entitles you to an unlimited number of journeys, day and night, within a 75-minute period. A 20-minute multi-journey ticket costs 3.40zł (€0.80) while a one-day travel card (zone 1) is 15zł (€3.50). Children under 7 travel for free.

Taxi: There are many licensed taxis waiting in line outside the airport's arrival hall with fares displayed on the side window or doors. A journey from Chopin airport to the city centre should not cost more than 40zł (€10) while from Modlin Airport – 100zł (€23.44). Avoid touts approaching you at the airports, train or bus stations offering illegal services who may charge you exorbitant fares for the journey. You can find a list of relia-

Child at the Chopin Museum

ble taxi companies on Warsaw airport's website (www.lotnisko-chopina.pl).

A good way to save money is the **Warsaw Pass** (www.warsawpass.com) valid for 24, 48 or 72 hours.

C

Children

Warsaw is a child-friendly city with many attractions that will delight little ones. All major museums now offer special educational programmes and have play areas designed with youngsters in mind. One of the best is the Copernicus Science Centre (www.kopernik.org.pl) where children can make their own discoveries and experiment during workshops and special programmes. There are also hands-on exhibits, planetarium shows, concerts, films, laboratory classes and lectures galore. The Warsaw Zoo (http://zoo.waw.pl) on the Vistula river right bank has always been a favourite place for family Sunday walks, but in recent years it has undergone a major transformation and now boasts excellent facilities too, sheltering around 4,000 animals and offering many educational programmes for children. Another good idea to keep children occupied is to take them to Łazienki Park, where they can take a boat ride on the lake, observe free roaming peacocks and swans or give hazel nuts to the red squirrels. Most young ones will also be thrilled to be whizzed up by a speedy lift to the Palace of Culture observation deck to have a look at the city spreading beneath their feet. In summer (May–Sept), the multimedia fountain park near the Old Town presents amazing music and laser shows, yet another children's favourite.

Clothing

The Polish climate is quite unpredictable (see page 12) so it's always wise to have a jumper and raincoat to hand. On the other hand, summers in Warsaw can also be suffocatingly hot, so pack light cottons if travelling at this time of the year. In winter, taking a warm coat, sturdy, water-resistant boots and wool trousers is advisable. People in Warsaw tend to be smart and style-conscious, so elegant clothes (jackets, dresses) are usually worn at special theatre or opera occasions, or when going to exclusive restaurants.

Crime and safety

Warsaw is a safe city and as far as visitors are concerned, the major crime is pickpocketing (usually on buses and trams) or car theft. Take the usual precautions, especially on trips to and from the airport (bus no.175 is notorious for pickpockets targeting tourists), at the railway station, and at night. Avoid less frequented and poorly-lit streets late at night, do not flash expensive jewellery or equipment in crowded places and you should be fine. Raucous football fans can sometimes be a problem before or after games of the local Legia team, but they rarely harass foreigners.

Warsaw police

Customs regulations

As a member of Schengen, Poland enacts EU regulations. Over 18s can import 800 cigarettes, 400 cigarillos, 200 cigars, 1kg of tobacco, 10 litres of spirits, 20 litres of fortified wine, 90 litres of wine and 110 litres of beer. Visitors from non-EU countries may bring a maximum of 1 litre of spirits, 4 litres of wine, 16 litres of beer, 200 cigarettes or 50 cigars or 250g of tobacco, without paying value added tax or custom duties. Sums exceeding €10,000 must be declared. There are strict regulations to prevent the export of objects of national heritage, such as works of art and antiques. For details, contact the Customs Information hotline (landline) at 801 470 477 or 33 857 62 51 (mobiles and from abroad).

Disabled travellers

A lot has been done in recent years to improve the situation for people with disabilities living in and visiting Warsaw. Many buses and trams now offer special ramps and spaces for wheelchair users, information screens, handles and signalling buttons. Low floor buses are indicated by square brackets on timetables (e.g. [10:22]) displayed at the bus stops. All modern pedestrian crossings are equipped with a system of sound signals and have ramps on footpaths. Most museums and parks, but not all public buildings, are accessible for disabled people, with ramps and lifts for wheelchairs. More information can be found at www.warsawtour.pl/en/niezb-dnik.html.

E

Electricity

The current is 220 volts AC, 50 Hertz throughout Poland. Plugs are the standard continental, round two-pin type. British and North American appliances need an adapter.

Embassies and consulates

Australia: Embassy, ul. Nowogrodzka 11, tel: 022 521 3444 (www.australia.pl).
Canada: Embassy, ul. Matejki 1/5, tel: 022 584 3100 (www.canadainternational.gc.ca/poland-pologne).
Ireland: Embassy (Warsaw), ul. Mysia 5, tel: 022 564 2200 (www.dfa.ie/irishembassy/poland).
New Zealand: Embassy, Al. Ujazdowskie 51, tel: 022 521 0500 (www.nzembassy.com/poland).
South Africa: Embassy (Warsaw), ul. Koszykowa 54, tel: 022 622 1005/1031 (www.dirco.gov.za/warsaw).
UK: Embassy, ul. Kawalerii 12, tel: 022 311 0000 (www.gov.uk/government/world/poland).
USA: Embassy, Al. Ujazdowskie 29/31, tel: 022 504 2000. (https://pl.usembassy.gov/pl).

Emergencies

General emergency number: 112
Police: 997

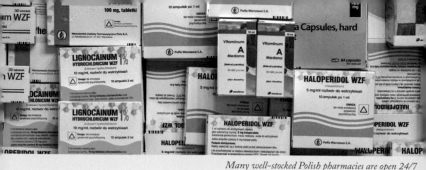

Many well-stocked Polish pharmacies are open 24/7

Fire brigade: 998
Ambulance: 999
Emergency numbers for foreigners in distress: tel: 800 200 300 or 608 599 999 (lines operate Jun–Sept 10am–10pm).

Etiquette

Poles are friendly and hospitable people. When invited to a Polish house, it is customary to bring a small gift – flowers (not chrysanthemums, though, which are reserved for funerals), sweets or a bottle of wine. It is considered polite to try a sample of each dish prepared by the hostess. Men greet each other with a firm handshake and women with three kisses on the cheek. Unless they are a good friend or partner, Polish men do not greet women with a kiss on the cheek (although this is also changing with so many Poles travelling to the Western countries) – a gentle handshake is more appropriate. The old custom of kissing a woman's hand is now nearly extinct and limited to the older generation. However, other forms of gallantry such as opening the doors and letting women pass first are still very common (although more contentious these days). On public transport, it is considered good manners to give up your seat to the elderly, pregnant women or disabled people.

G

Gay and lesbian travellers

Even though homosexuality is legal in Poland, many people hold conserva-tive attitudes and do not openly tolerate it. Public displays of affection may be greeted with hostility and so should be avoided. Lambda (ul. Żurawia 24A, tel: 022 628 5222, www.lambdawarszawa. org) is a good source of information on Warsaw's quickly changing gay scene. Alternatively, check www.travel gayeurope.com/warsaw-gay-bars or http://warsaw.gayguide.net.

H

Health

Polish doctors and other health officials are generally knowledgeable and skilled, and most speak some English. Medical treatment will normally be provided free of charge to EU citizens who have a European Health Insurance Card (available from post offices in the UK and online at www.ehic.org. uk). Visitors from non-EU countries should obtain medical insurance, and even EU citizens may wish to insure themselves privately, for example to ensure prompt repatriation in a medical emergency.

Vaccinations: The Centers for Disease Control and Prevention (CDC) recommend that all routine vaccines are up-to-date when travelling to Poland.

Water: It is now safe to drink tap water in Warsaw.

Pharmacies: Look for the sign 'Apteka'. In Poland these shops only sell pharmaceutical and related products. There are many 24-hour pharmacies across town;

Corpus Christi procession

you can find their list at www.warsaw-tour.pl.

Private hospitals

Centrum Medyczne Damiana, Wałbrzyska 46, tel: 022 566 22 22; www.damian.pl

Enel Med Szpital Zacisze, Gilarska 86c, tel: 022 23 07 007, 0660 307 007; https://enel.pl

Lux Med., Puławska 455, tel: 22 431 20 59; www.luxmed.pl/szpital.html

Medicover, Rzeczypospolitej 5, tel: 500 900 900, 500 900 901; www.medicover.pl/szpital

Hours and holidays

Most businesses in Poland are usually open Monday to Friday 8am–5pm, but these times may vary. Supermarkets, department stores and shopping centres are open daily 10am–9pm (some even later). Smaller shops usually stay open from 7am–7pm Mon–Fri, and until 2pm on Sat. Banks are generally open 8am–6pm Monday to Friday; branches in shopping centres are open the same as the centres. Museums hours vary, but most are open 10am–5pm Tuesday to Sunday.

Public holidays:

1 January New Year's Day
6 January Epiphany
March/April Easter Sunday and Easter Monday
1 May Labour Day
3 May Constitution Day
May/June Pentecost (7th Sunday after Easter)
June Corpus Christi (9th Thursday after Easter)
15 August Feast of the Assumption
1 November All Saints' Day
11 November Independence Day
25 December Christmas Day
26 December St Stephen's Day

Internet facilities

Free WiFi is widely available in hotels, cafés, shopping centres and many parts of the city including the Old Town, Krakowskie Przedmieście and Nowy Świat streets. A map of free WiFi coverage can be found at www.warsawtour.pl.

L

Language

Polish is one of the most difficult languages to learn. Fortunately, many Poles (particularly younger) can easily communicate in English. See page 134 for a glossary of Polish words and phrases.

M

Media

Newspapers and magazines. The *Warsaw Voice* (www.warsawvoice.pl), published weekly, is probably the most authoritative English-language newspaper. It gives a good insight into Polish politics, business and culture and also has a listings section for tourists. Other

papers to look for include *Welcome to Warsaw* (a free information magazine), *Warsaw Insider* (www.warsawinsider.pl) a free monthly with cultural listings, Culture.pl, an authoritative online guide to Polish culture, and the *In Your Pocket* mini-guides, which have lots of listings. Visitor.pl (www.thevisitor.pl) is an online guide with a separate section dedicated to Warsaw. Western newspapers, including *The International Herald Tribune*, *The Financial Times*, *The Guardian* and *USA Today* arrive on the day of publication. Others may arrive a day or two late.

Radio and television. Polskie Radio (www.thenews.pl) is transmitted in English, streamed over the internet and as podcasts. Even quite modest hotels now offer satellite television with major European and American channels and news programmes.

Money

Currency. The unit of currency is the złoty (zł). Coins in circulation include 1, 2 and 5 zł. Banknotes come in denominations of 10, 20, 50, 100, 200 and 500 (recently introduced). One złoty equals 100 groszy (gr), which you'll see in 1, 2, 5, 10, 20 and 50 coin denominations. You can pay in euros at some supermarkets and shops.

Currency exchange. Foreign currency can be exchanged at the airports and banks, as well as most hotels and commercial centres (look for the sign 'Kantor'). Kantors only exchange cash and can be very informal-looking places. They offer the best rates (no commission). The exchange rate at the time of writing is around 4.2zł to the euro and 3.75zł to the US dollar. There is no black market for currency in Poland; refuse any offers from strangers on the street. The Polish word for cash is 'gotówka'.

ATMs and credit cards. The Polish word for ATM is 'bankomat'. They are numerous (over a thousand in Warsaw), conveniently located and accept all major international cards including American Express, Cirrus, MasterCard, Visa, Visa Electron and Maestro. These are also widely accepted at most establishments across town.

Travellers cheques. These may be cashed at most banks and at the airport but not at kantors.

P

Post

Branches of Poczta Polska (Polish Post) are usually open Mon–Fri from 8am–8pm, some also on Sat and Sun. The Central Post Office in Warsaw (Świętokrzyska 31–33, tel: 022 505 3534) is open daily 24 hours. Letter boxes are red and usually located outside post offices. A stamp for a standard letter/postcard sent abroad currently costs 5zł. It usually arrives within three days, or the next day in case of a priority letter (extra fee applies). More information at www.poczta-polska.pl.

WPT1313 tour car

R

Religion

The dominant religion in Poland is Catholicism. Even though 92 percent of Poles identify themselves as Catholics, only 39 percent regularly attend Sunday Mass. There are also small Protestant, Jewish and Muslim communities. Addresses of churches of different faiths can be found at http://warsawtour.pl. Traditionally, Poles have been very tolerant toward other religions, but recently, the Polish government's hard stance on immigration has galvanised nationalist circles that vociferously oppose the arrival of migrants from Muslim countries.

S

Smoking and drinking

Smoking is forbidden at bus stops and in pubs, restaurants and clubs unless there is a separate room for smokers. It is forbidden to drink alcohol in public places such as parks, squares and streets.

T

Telephones

The area code for Warsaw is 22, and it must be dialled even when making local calls. To call Warsaw from abroad, dial the country code, +48, followed by the rest of the number. When calling abroad from Warsaw dial '00', the international code and then the number. Public pay-phones are now very rare and in most cases accept pre-paid telephone cards or, less often, coins.

Mobile phones. As of June 2017, mobile users from elsewhere in the EU are benefitting from the abolition of roaming charges. Other visitors can avoid roaming costs by buying a local, prepaid SIM card for their mobile phone. Several companies offer cheap start-up packages which can be bought from shops and kiosks around the city. However, due to security reasons, all SIM cards must now be activated at one of the operator's offices (bring your ID or passport). The country's main mobile phone operators are Orange, T-Mobile, Play and Plus.
International dialling codes:
Australia **61**
Canada **1**
Ireland **353**
UK **44**
US **1**

Time zones

Warsaw is one hour ahead of the GMT in the Central European Time zone. As in the rest of Europe, the clocks go forward one hour on the last Sunday of March (summer time) and back again on the last Sunday of October (winter time).

Tipping

Note that a 10 percent tip in recognition of good service is expected at all but the cheapest restaurants (only a few automatically add service to the bill, particularly when the group is large).

Warsaw's Chopin Airport

Toilets

In Warsaw public toilets (*toaleta*) can be few and far between. A small charge (usually 2zł) is common. Cafés and restaurants will also make their toilets available for those in need (though it is recommended to buy something to avoid glares). You will find toilets in all commercial centres and in most petrol stations. Men's rooms are commonly denoted by triangle symbols; women's rooms are denoted by circles.

Tourist information

You will find tourist information points at Chopin Airport (Arrivals hall); the Palace of Culture and Science (pl. Defilad 1); The Central Railway Station's main hall; Old Town's Square. All are open 9am–6pm. You can find more information at www.warsawtour.pl.

Tours and guides

Adventure Warsaw, Mińska 25, tel: 606 22 55 25; http://adventurewarsaw.pl – popular 'off the beaten path' tours centred on the communist past.
City Sightseeing Warsaw, Emilii Plater, tel: 793 95 79 79; www.city-sightseeing.pl – the familiar red double-decker hop-on hop-off cruises taking in major sights.
Station Warsaw, King Sigimund's Column in the Old Town; tel: 661 36 87 58; www.stationwarsaw.com – organises various thematic cycle tours. Prior booking essential.
Eat Polska, tel: 661 36 87 58; www.

eatpolska.com – discover Polish cuisine with these excellent gastro tours.
WPT1313, tel: 22 882 1313; www.wpt1313.com – various tours 'on the trail of Polish communis' in the legendary Fiat 126p cars painted yellow like New York cabs.

Transport

By air

International flights arrive and depart from the Warsaw Chopin Airport (Żwirki i Wigury 1; www.lotnisko-chopina.pl), southwest of the capital. It is well-connected with most cities in Europe as well as several US airports (New York, Chicago, LA) and served by all major airlines including Polish Airlines LOT, British Airways, Lufthansa, Air France, KLM and American Airlines. It is located 8km (5 miles) or about 30 minutes away from the city centre. A **taxi** should cost no more than 40zł. Some of the taxis waiting out front may look official, but are not and will charge exorbitant prices, so be careful. Avoid taxi drivers offering their services inside the terminal.

If you need to take a taxi, call for one at the information desk: Ele Taxi (tel: 022 811 1111), Sawa Taxi (tel: 022 644 4444) or Super Taxi (tel: 022 196-22/196-61). Three **buses** run daily from 5am–11pm from the airport. The no.175 stops at Dworzec Centralny (the main train station), while the no.148 goes to South Praga, and the no.188 passes Metro Politechnika in the city centre. No.331 (Mon–Fri until 6pm) passes

Warszawa Centralna station

Metro Wilanowska and the N32 night bus gets you to the main railway station.

Trains operated by SKM (Fast Urban Railway; www.skm.warszawa.pl) and Koleje Mazowieckie (www.mazowieckie.com.pl) leave every 15 minutes from the underground station adjacent to the airport terminal. Line S2 goes to Warszawa Śródmieście (city centre) and S3 to the Warszawa Wschodnia railway terminal across the Vistula river. Koleje Mazowieckie offer connections to Modlin airport (a shuttle bus operates between the terminal and the railway station).

Opened in 2012, **Modlin airport** (WMI; Gen. Wiktora Thommee 1a, Nowy Dwór Mazowiecki; www.modlinairport.pl) is situated about 40km (25 miles) north of Warsaw. It's a modern hub for low-cost carriers including Ryanair and Wizzair. Koleje Mazowieckie and Modlin shuttle bus (www.modlinbus.pl) operate regular services between the city centre and the airport.

By car

Warsaw is best approached from the west through the A2 motorway linking it with Poznań and, further, Berlin. Other international roads leading to Warsaw include: E77 (North-West), E67 (North-East), E30 (East), E77 (South-West).

By coach

Most regional and long-distance coaches including Eurolines, Ecolines, and Simple Express arrive at Dworzec Warszawa Zachodnia (Al. Jerozolimskie 144; https://dworzeconline.pl). Some private bus companies, including PolskiBus (www.polskibus.com) serving national and international destinations, leave from Wilanowska Metro Station.

By train

Most international trains leave and arrive at Warszawa Centralna railway station (Al. Jerozolimskie 54; tel: 22 474 40 86; http://pkpsa.pl) with regular connections to Berlin, Prague, Ostrava, Vienna, Bratislava, Budapest, Moscow and Kiev.

Public transport

Public transport in Warsaw (www.ztm-warszawa.pl) is safe, efficient and punctual. There are two zones: 1 (comprising the city and the airport) and 2 (far-out suburbs and satellite towns). Don't forget to validate your ticket once you get on the bus or tram.

Buses. Hundreds of buses ply Warsaw streets between 5am and 11pm. There are regular lines (three digits) which stop on every marked stop, accelerated ones (beginning with 4xx and 5xx and red-marked), express lines (E-x, also marked in red) operating at peak hours on weekdays, suburban lines (beginning with 7xx or 8xx) and night buses (Nxx) operating every 30 minutes between 11.15pm and 4.30am, which leave from a bus stop near Central Railway Station. The most useful line for tourists is no.180 (see page 15). Tickets can be bought at kiosks, ticket machines, some shops and from the driver (bus/tram). They are

Taking Veturilo bikes for a spin

also valid for the metro. The standard single ticket for Zone 1 is valid for 75 minutes and includes unlimited transfers for 4.40zł (€1.04). Cheaper 20-minute tickets cost 3.40zł (€0.80). There are also 24-hour and 3-day tickets on offer. More information on prices and timetables can be found at www.ztm-warszawa.pl.

Metro. The most modern in Europe, the Warsaw metro currently has two lines: M1 connects Młociny (in the north of the city) with Kabaty (in the south) while the currently expanded M2 line links the western (Wola) and eastern part of the city (Praga) under the Vistula River. The metro runs daily between 5am and midnight (every 3–4 minutes during peak hours, every 7–8 minutes off-peak) and until 2.30am on Fri–Sat (every 15 minutes after midnight).

Trains. The SKM (Rapid Urban Railway) and Koleje Mazowieckie (Mazovian Railways) connect the city with suburbs and nearby towns.

Trams. Trams have numbers below 50 and are the best way to move around the congested city centre on weekdays. A special T route with historic cars operates from Narutowicza Square in July–August. For details see www.ztm.waw.pl.

City bike scheme (Veturilo). The city bike system called Vetirulo consists of more than 300 stations and over 4,600 bikes. The first 20 minutes are free. It is an efficient and pleasant way to move around the city. All details including the map of the stations are available at www.veturilo.waw.pl/en.

V

Visas and passports

EU passport-holders and visitors from the US, Canada, Australia and New Zealand do not need a visa to enter Poland; a valid passport (at least for the proposed duration of your stay) or ID is sufficient.

W

Websites

www.um.warszawa.pl/en – the official city of Warsaw website

www.warsawtour.pl – the city of Warsaw's official tourist guide

www.warsawguide.com – exhaustive Warsaw city guide in English

www.culture.pl – comprehensive about Polish culture and current events

www.ztm.waw.pl – the official website of the Warsaw public transport system with an excellent route planner and up to date timetables.

Weights and measures

Poland uses the metric system.

Women travellers

Women travelling alone will find Warsaw an easy-going, non-threatening place to explore. However, the usual precautions should be taken: avoid walking alone late at night and do not flash expensive jewellery or electronic equipment, especially in crowded areas where pickpockets tend to operate.

LANGUAGE

Polish, a Slavic language, is the mother tongue of 99 percent of the population. The Polish language is grammatically complicated, but at least it is written completely phonetically. Learning even a handful of key phrases is a good idea and will prove helpful. As a general rule, the accent falls on the second-last syllable. The following are a few useful phrases and some signs you are likely to see.

Useful phrases

Hi/bye Cześć
Yes Tak
No Nie
Thank you Dziękuje
Please Proszę
Good morning /afternoon Dzień dobry
Good evening Dobry wieczór
Goodbye Do widzenia
Sorry/Excuse me Przepraszam
I would like... Chciałbym (men)/Chciałabym (women)
Where is...? Gdzie jest?
How far? Jak daleko?
How long? Jak długo?
OK Dobrze
Cheap Tanio
Expensive Drogo
Hot Gorąco
Cold Zimno
Free Wolny
Occupied Zajęty
I don't understand Nie rozumiem
Help! Pomocy!

Signs

Open Otwarte
Closed Zamknięte
Exit Wyjście
Pharmacy Apteka
Post Office Poczta
Avenue Aleja (al)
Street ulica (ul)
Old Town Stare Miasto
Police Station Posterunek Policji
Information Informacja
Toilets/WC Toalety
Men Panowie
Women Panie
No Smoking Palenie Wzbronione
Cash Desk Kasa

Numbers

zero zero
one jeden
two dwa / dwie
three trzy
four cztery
five pięć
six sześć
seven siedem
eight osiem
nine dziewięć
ten dziesięć
eleven jedenaście
fifteen piętnaście
sixteen szesnaście
seventeen siedemnaście
eighteen osiemnaście
nineteen dziewiętnaście

Get a basic grasp of common Polish words you will see out and about

twenty *dwadzieścia*
thirty *trzydzieści*
forty *czterdzieści*
fifty *pięćdziesiąt*
hundred *sto*

Days of the week

Monday *Poniedziałek*
Tuesday *Wtorek*
Wednesday *Środa*
Thursday *Czwartek*
Friday *Piątek*
Saturday *Sobota*
Sunday *Niedziela*

Online

Is there a wireless internet? *Czy jest tu bezprzewodowy internet?*
What is the WiFi password? *Jakie jest hasło do sieci WiFi?*
Is the WiFi free? *Czy WiFi jest płatne?*
Can I ....? *Czy mogę....*
access the internet? *podłączyć się do internetu?*
plug in/charge my laptop/iPhone/ iPad? *naładować laptopa/iPhone'a/ iPada?*
What's your e-mail? *Jaki masz e-mail?*

Social media

Are you on Facebook? *Jesteś na Facebooku?*
What's your user name? *Jaki masz pseudonim/Jakiego masz nicka?*
I'll add you as a friend *Dodam cię do przyjaciół*
I'll follow you on Twitter *Będę cię obserwował na Twitterze*

I'll put the pictures on Facebook/Twitter/Instagram *Zamieszczę zdjęcia na Facebooku/Twitterze/Instagramie.*

Shopping

How much is it? *Ile to kosztuje?*
I would like to buy... *Chciałbym/Chciałabym kupić...*
Do you take credit cards? *Przyjmujecie karty kredytowe?*
I'm just looking *Tylko oglądam*
What size? *Jaki rozmiar?*
Too big *Za duże*
Too small *Za małe*
Perfect *Idealne*
Receipt *Paragon*
Invoice *Rachunek*
Pharmacy - *Apteka*
Bakery *Piekarnia*
Book shop *Księgarnia*
Patisserie *Cukiernia*
Department store *Sklep wielobranżowy*
Market *Targ*
Supermarket *Supermarket*

Dining out

breakfast *śniadanie*
lunch *lunch/obiad*
dinner *kolacja*
meal *posiłek*
first course *pierwsze danie*
main course *drugie danie*
the bill *rachunek*
I am a vegetarian *Jestem wegetarianinem/wegetarianką*
I'd like to order *Chciał(a)bym zamówić*
Enjoy your meal! *Smacznego!*
tip *napiwek*

A POLISH FILM OF UNIQUE
TENSION AND POWER

KANAL
(X)

A story of the heroic Warsaw Rising

'Kanał' poster

BOOKS AND FILM

Books

With its sombre history, diverse culture and mixed population, Warsaw has provided a rich backdrop and an inspiration for literary works of giants of Polish literature from Adam Mickiewicz to Sylwia Chutnik. Warsaw witnessed the most tragic events in Poland's modern history and, unsurprisingly, the city has been an infinite source of inspiration for generations of Polish writers. Below is just a selection of some books translated into English which offer a glimpse into Warsaw's and Poland's history, its culture and people's mindsets.

History, society and culture:
Between East and West by Anne Applebaum. US journalist's account of her travels through Poland.
Jewish Roots in Poland: Pages from the Past and Archival Inventories by Miriam Weiner. The most comprehensive guide to Polish Jewry.
Atlas of Warsaw's Architecture by J.A. Chrościcki and A. Rottermund. Interesting and informative atlas of Warsaw's architectural treasures.
Polish National Cinema by Marek Haltof. A comprehensive study of Polish Cinema from the end of the 19th century to the present.
The Jews in Poland by Chimen Abramsky, Maciej Jachimczyk and Anthony Polonsky. Comprehensive historical background of the Jewish community in Poland.
Heart of Europe: A Short History of Poland by Norman Davies. Balanced and entertaining history from World War II onwards.
The Polish Way by Adam Zamoyski. An accessible history of Poland up to the 1989 elections.
Rising '44 by Norman Davies. Gripping account of the Warsaw Uprising.
Warsaw 1944: Hitler, Himmler and the Crushing of a City by Alexandra Richie. Using first-hand accounts, the author retells this tragic moment in the city's history from both German and Polish perspectives.
Winter in the Morning by Janina Bauman. A survivor's moving account of life in the Warsaw Ghetto.
A Memoir of the Warsaw Uprising by Miron Białoszewski. A first-hand, faithful albeit anti-heroic account of a 63-day long struggle.
The History of Polish Literature by Czesław Miłosz. Written in the 1960s, this is still one of the most comprehensive books on Polish literature.

Fiction:
The Doll by Bolesław Prus. One of the greatest Polish novels of all times, this offers a detailed portrait of the quickly developing city and its inhabitants at the end of 19th century.
A Minor Apocalypse by Tadeusz Kon-

wicki. One of the best known Polish underground books, this is a poignant picture of socialist Warsaw in the 1980s. **The Man With White Eyes** by Leopold Tyrmand. Set in the post-war Warsaw crime world, this best seller novel was considered by many as a symbol of the political thaw in the Polish literature.
Entaglement by Zygmunt Miłoszewski. Set in Warsaw, this is the first part of the trilogy featuring prosecutor Teodor Szacki, the Polish version of Kurt Wallander.

Film

The communist authorities highly valued the propaganda effect of cinema, so soon after World War II they set up a centre of cinematography in Łódź, 140km (87 miles) southwest of the destroyed Warsaw. In the 1950s, Polish film was bound by Socialist style, with no room for originality. Only after Stalin's death in 1953, did it become possible to make films that did not reflect communist propaganda clichés and the Polish Film School emerged. The late Andrzej Wajda and Roman Polański were the most prominent figures of this new generation of filmmakers. Today, the school in Łódź continues to spawn talented directors (and cameramen) including Wojciech Smarzowski (*The Wedding, Dark House*) and Małgorzata Szumowska (*33 Scenes From Life, Sponsoring*).
Kanał (1956). Andrzej Wajda's dark, depressing drama depicts the last days of the Warsaw Uprising from the perspective of a battered Home Army unit ordered to take to the sewers to cross German lines.
Giusseppe w Warszawie (*Giusseppe in Warsaw*, 1964). A hilarious comedy set in German-occupied Warsaw with a plethora of famous Polish actors.
The Pianist (2002). Roman Polański won a Best Director Academy Award for this deeply personal film, the real-life story of a Jewish pianist, Władysław Szpilman (played by Oscar-winning Adrien Brody), who miraculously survived the annihilation of the Warsaw Ghetto.
Rezerwat (2007). Łukasz Pałkowski's film is a story about life in contemporary Praga, seen through the eyes of the inhabitants – including a promising young photographer – of a ruined townhouse on Konopacka street.
Drogówka (Traffic Department, 2011). Directed by Wojciech Smarzowski and set in contemporary Warsaw, this exposes the corruption and shady deals of the capital's policemen.
Miasto 44 (*Warsaw 44*, 2014). Jan Komasa directs a modern, unorthodox take on the Warsaw Uprising in which the horrors of the war are shown through eyes of a pair of young lovers.
Powstanie Warszawskie (*The Warsaw Uprising*, 2014). A moving, remastered compilation of documentary films recorded by Polish insurgents showing scenes from the Warsaw Uprising.
Wszystkie nieprzespane noce (*All These Sleepless Nights*, 2016). Warsaw's vibrant nightlife is skilfully revealed by Michał Marczak, the Sundance Film Festival 2016's best director.

ABOUT THIS BOOK

This *Explore Guide* has been produced by the editors of Insight Guides, whose books have set the standard for visual travel guides since 1970. With top-quality photography and authoritative recommendations, these guidebooks bring you the very best routes and itineraries in the world's most exciting destinations.

BEST ROUTES

The routes in the book provide something to suit all budgets, tastes and trip lengths. As well as covering the destination's many classic attractions, the itineraries track lesser-known sights, and there are also excursions for those who want to extend their visit outside the city centre. The routes embrace a range of interests, so whether you are an art fan, a gourmet, a history buff or have kids to entertain, you will find an option to suit.

We recommend reading the whole of a route before setting out. This should help you to familiarise yourself with it and enable you to plan where to stop for refreshments – options are shown in the 'Food and Drink' box at the end of each tour.

For our pick of the tours by theme, consult Recommended Routes for… (see pages 6–7).

INTRODUCTION

The routes are set in context by this introductory section, giving an overview of the destination to set the scene, plus background information on food and drink, shopping and more, while a succinct history timeline highlights the key events over the centuries.

DIRECTORY

Also supporting the routes is a Directory chapter, with a clearly organised A–Z of practical information, our pick of where to stay while you are there and select restaurant listings; these eateries complement the more low-key cafés and restaurants that feature within the routes and are intended to offer a wider choice for evening dining. Also included here are some nightlife listings, plus a handy language guide and our recommendations for books and films about the destination.

ABOUT THE AUTHORS

Explore Warsaw was written by husband-and-wife team Maciej Zglinicki and Natalia Zglinicka. A third-generation Varsovian, Maciej is a freelance journalist, editor and translator working with Polish and foreign media outlets, including the BBC World Service in Warsaw and London. Natalia, a graduate of History of Art at the University of Warsaw, has been following Warsaw's amazing transformation from a neglected and depressing communist city into the bustling metropolis of today for many years. Her areas of interest include modern art and architecture.

CONTACT THE EDITORS

We hope you find this Explore Guide useful, interesting and a pleasure to read. If you have any questions or feedback on the text, pictures or maps, please do let us know. If you have noticed any errors or outdated facts, or have suggestions for places to include on the routes, we would be delighted to hear from you. Please drop us an email at hello@insightguides.com. Thanks!

CREDITS

Explore Warsaw
Editor: Sarah Clark
Author: Maciej Zglinicki and Natalia Zglinicka
Head of Production: Rebeka Davies
Update Production: Apa Digital
Picture Editor: Tom Smyth
Cartography: Carte
Photo credits: 4Corners Images 8/9T;
Adrian Grycuk 34/35, 75L; Alamy 7T, 16,
17, 18, 19L, 18/19, 23, 25, 53, 57, 58, 72,
74/75, 77, 83, 84/85, 94, 95, 96, 97L,
96/97, 98, 99, 102, 104, 122, 123, 137;
Alik Keplicz/AP/REX/Shutterstock 108B;
Bartlomiej Zborowski/Epa/REX/Shutter-
stock 22; Czarek Sokolowski/AP/REX/Shut-
terstock 80/81, 103, 108T, 109; Design Hotels 114; Dyspensa 120; fotokon 61L; Getty
Images 6BC, 41, 54/55, 67, 76, 101B, 129,
136; Gregory Wrona/Apa Publications 131,
134/135; Grzegorz Jakubowski/Epa/REX/
Shutterstock 24; iStock 1, 4ML, 4MC, 6ML,
7MR, 8ML, 8MC, 8ML, 10, 11, 14/15, 20,
21L, 20/21, 28ML, 28MC, 32, 35L, 52,
66, 124, 126, 132; Leonardo 6TL, 110MR,
110ML, 115; Leszek Szymanski/Epa/REX/
Shutterstock 82; Marcus Lindstrom 60/61;
Muzeum Warszawy 4MC, 8MR, 28MC,
28ML, 36; Piotr Haltof/Restauracja Polska
Różana 119; Polska Organizacja Turystyczna
125, 133; Public domain 26, 27, 88/89;
Radek Pietrusszka/Epa/REX/Shutterstock
70; Robert Harding 110/111T; Shutterstock
4MR, 4MR, 4ML, 6MC, 7MR, 7M, 8MC,
8MR, 12, 13L, 12/13, 28MR, 28MR, 30,
33, 34, 37, 39, 40, 42, 43L, 42/43, 44/45,
47, 48, 49L, 48/49, 50, 51, 54, 55L, 56,
59L, 58/59, 60, 62/63, 64, 68/69, 71,
73, 74, 78, 79L, 78/79, 80, 84, 85L, 87,
90, 91, 93, 100, 101T, 105, 106, 107L,
106/107, 127, 128, 130; Starwood Hotels
& Resorts 110ML, 110MC, 110MR, 110MC,
112, 113, 116, 117, 118; Stary Dom 121;
SuperStock 4/5T, 28/29T, 31, 38, 46, 65,
81L, 86, 92
Cover credits: iStock (main & bottom)

Printed by CTPS – China

DISTRIBUTION

UK, Ireland and Europe
Apa Publications (UK) Ltd
sales@insightguides.com
United States and Canada
Ingram Publisher Services
ips@ingramcontent.com
Australia and New Zealand
Woodslane
info@woodslane.com.au
Southeast Asia
Apa Publications (Singapore) Pte
singaporeoffice@insightguides.com
Hong Kong, Taiwan and China
Apa Publications (HK) Ltd
hongkongoffice@insightguides.com
Worldwide
Apa Publications (UK) Ltd
sales@insightguides.com

SPECIAL SALES, CONTENT LICENSING AND COPUBLISHING

Insight Guides can be purchased in bulk
quantities at discounted prices. We can
create special editions, personalised jackets
and corporate imprints tailored to your needs.
sales@insightguides.com
www.insightguides.biz

INDEX